FAITH ISN'T SAFE, REBELLION IS BORING, AND COWARDS WON'T INHERIT THE KINGDOM.

KILLER
church

VOLUME II

NATHAN FINOCHIO

Contents

To the Alessi Family,
who encouraged
the writing of this book.

Chapter One

Young and Old

"In many ways, the work of a critic is easy. We risk very little, yet enjoy a position over those who offer up their work and their selves to our judgment. We thrive on negative criticism, which is fun to write and to read. But the bitter truth we critics must face is that, in the grand scheme of things, the average piece of junk is probably more meaningful than our criticism designating it so. But there are times when a critic truly risks something, and that is in the discovery and defense of the 'new.' The world is often unkind to a new talent, new creations. The new needs friends."
—Anton Ego, *Ratatouille*

I like Gen Z as much as I like any other generation. To be quite honest, I love the energy, the brashness, and the naïveté of youth. And not in a hollow, performative sense, but in the purest form of youth—that fascination with the new, that ability to see possibilities invisible to those who have grown too accustomed to the old.

But here's the thing: everything is new to them. Even old things are new. And there is something profoundly **Divine** in that.

Chesterton once suggested that **God has stayed young while we have grown old.** He paints a picture of God as fresh as the newest flower, always celebrating and sustaining creation in a way we humans struggle to grasp. He is, paradoxically, both the Ancient of Days and forever young.

This is why I believe it is the critic's job to **celebrate** the new.

And let's remember: a film critic doesn't hate movies—he loves them. Nobody becomes a food critic because they despise sustenance. Quite the opposite. **Critics are obsessives.** They are deeply fixated on the things they keenly observe and review.

I am a **church critic** because I love the Church. She is **beautiful** in my eyes—and in the eyes of Christ.

And part of my job as a critic—one whose careful eyes are motivated by nothing more than heartfelt appreciation—is to **celebrate what is new** while keeping two feet planted in the greatest traditions that made the thing sublime in the first place.

A film critic knows that *Casablanca, To Kill a Mockingbird, Lawrence of Arabia,* and *The Godfather* are part of the canon. It is from **the canon** that new things are appreciated and critiqued.

So as someone who loves **Scripture** and loves the **Church**—both **ancient** and **Spirit-born** works—I believe it is my duty to almost **defend the new.** To defend and celebrate the methodological contributions that **each young generation brings** to the household of faith.

Their music is going to be different.

And as long as the **biblical principles of worship are embraced,** I ought not only to **defend** their music—I ought to **enjoy** it.

Because it's not enough for me to simply **defend** their methods.

Not if I want to be like **my Creator, who is young.**

I must **strain** to enjoy their fresh expressions.

I do **not** want to be **older than God.**

That is the posture I'm supposed to take toward the generation below me.

So, yeah, I'm **pushing for fellowship with them.** I'm **including** them in what I do. I'm **making room** for them and their many foreign iterations of Christian life. I'm **learning how they speak**—I'm going **full immersion.**

They aren't a **problem**—they're a **blessing.**

They aren't to be **endured**—they're to be **enjoyed.**

And now, here's where I **flip the script: I don't think revival belongs exclusively to youth.**

Hear me out.

I'm not coming after **revivals** or **revivalists** or **moves of the Spirit.** I'm **open.** I'm **hungry.** I **love** it when youth and young adults **chase after the things of God.** History tells us that some of the most powerful movements of faith have been driven by fiery **college students**—unshaken by fear, undeterred by tradition, ready to **risk everything** for conviction.

We **need** those voices.

But the more I read **Scripture**, the more I see a **pattern**—and the more I look at how **Pentecostals** and **Charismatics** define revival, the more I wonder:

How much of our **modern definition of revival** is just the **cultural idol of youth** sneaking into **Christian thought?**

Because **youth** as an idol **isn't new.** In fact, it's **ancient.**

One of the **oldest** human stories we'll examine in this book (*spoiler alert: we're going deep into the Babel narrative*) is exactly that—the **youth of the world uniting** in an attempt to **solve spiritual problems.**

But this isn't just a commentary on youth.

It's about **the world itself**—banding together, believing it can **fix itself** through sheer **willpower and synergy.**

And what do we see woven through **modern Secularism?**

That same **theme**—the **hope** of a **human-engineered utopia.**

The original audience listening to **Moses** recount the story of **Babel** might not have immediately recognized the **folly of youth** in the tale. But what comes **right after it**, in **Genesis 12**, makes it glaringly obvious.

Because when **God** decided to **enact Salvation History**, He didn't **pick the brightest, youngest innovators**.

He picked three **washed-up**, **old**, **forgotten nobodies**:

- **Noah** saved **humanity** physically.
- **Abraham** saved **humanity** spiritually.
- **Moses** saved **God's people** both **physically** and **spiritually**.

And **Moses's case**? Absolutely **fascinating**.

The Gospel According to Lawrence of Arabia

When I was a kid, I was **obsessed** with *Lawrence of Arabia*.

Not casually interested. **Obsessed**.

Because I was **that** kid—the oddball. The eccentric. The one who **never quite fit in** with the others. A fact I learned through that **sacred childhood rite of passage: bullying.**

I went from being a **kind**, **openhearted** boy to a **walled-off**, **self-conscious** boy.

And here's the **tragic irony**: the very **skillsets** my mother **equipped me with**—singing loudly, making up **silly songs**, expressing myself **creatively**—became **fuel** for the fire of ridicule.

I learned **quickly** that I didn't have the **right tool belt** to navigate **school life**.

So I adapted.

I took my **quirkiness** and **honesty**, and I **weaponized them**.

I trained myself to be the **fastest, sharpest**, and **most cutting** in the verbal jungle.

I remember the moment I **flipped the switch**—standing there, **eviscerated** by the **older boys**, deciding right then and there:

If I can't win, I'll be better at losing.

I became an **expert** at memorizing **slanders** and **personalized sneers**.

And then, at **3:30 p.m.**, the bell rang.

Mum picked me up from school, and the armor **came off**.

I was **her** silly, gentle boy again.

My father rented **old movies**—almost **exclusively**.

We grew up watching **black-and-white, pre-code Hollywood films**—family-friendly by **default**.

On **Saturdays**, Mum took us to the **Hamilton Public Library**, where we **raided** the free movie rentals. (*I think you could take out* ***ten at a time***, *which was dangerously close to* ***heaven*** *for me.*)

And one **Saturday afternoon**, my **nine-year-old** hands grabbed something that would **change me**:

Lawrence of Arabia—starring **Peter O'Toole**.

A film about a **weird, brilliant, outcast British officer** who somehow led an **Arab revolt** against the Turks in **World War I**.

And something in me **clicked**.

I couldn't **articulate it** at the time, but I **knew**:

I was **Lawrence**.

I was **the man on the motorcycle**, speeding recklessly through the **English countryside**.

I was the **distracted, head-in-the-clouds, misunderstood dreamer** who could do **great things**—but not within the **strictures** of our **Baptist-curriculum fishbowl**.

Our clip-on ties and collegiate cardigans? **My handcuffs.**

And the rest of the students? **The rank-and-file officers in the mess hall**, writing me off as an **idiot**.

I watched that movie **religiously**.

My mother did some digging and discovered that **T. E. Lawrence** had written extensively about his adventures with the Bedouin in a **large-print tome** titled *Seven Pillars of Wisdom*. I remember renting it from the library and **lapping it up like a puppy.**

One particularly interesting section of **Lawrence's recollections**—so raw and **out-of-pocket** for the **sheltered Christian boy** that I was—described what he observed among the **shepherd boys** of the region.

Shepherding, even at this late period in history, was relegated to **societal outcasts**. And Lawrence writes about how **backward** and **incapable of speech** these men became after spending **two to three months** alone with their flocks. The long solitude rendered them almost **mute**, barely able to **interact with people.**

And then came the part I'll **never forget**—because it was the **first vulgarity** I had ever read.

Lawrence sketches out the **sexual practices** of these shepherds, who were **known to bugger the sheep they herded.**

Yep. You read that right.

I remember staring at the page, my **nine-year-old** mind scrambling to **process this new and horrifying revelation.**

Moses, the Silent Shepherd

Moses spends **forty years** not just **unlearning Egypt**—but **unlearning everything**.

Keep in mind: **shepherding was an abomination to the Egyptians.**

And perhaps, just like **those Bedouin shepherds**, Moses' **inability to speak** stemmed from the same cause. Maybe he had spent **so much time** talking to **sheep** that he'd lost the ability to **talk to people.**

Because, let's be honest—sheep **don't** make great conversation partners.

Moses is **eighty years old and regressed.**

He's the **decrepit Model T**, abandoned in some overgrown country field, buried in **wild grass and rust**.

And when I read about **Moses' forty years of decay** on the **Sinai Peninsula**—his own **admission** that he had **lost his fast-ball**—I immediately recalled those **Bedouin shepherds**. The **psychological toll** of that kind of isolation.

But here's where things get interesting:

Was Moses' honest **self-adjudication** frustrating to **YHWH**, or was it meant to **send a message** to the hearers?

Because maybe—just maybe—**God wanted Moses to die out**.

Or rather—He wanted Moses to reach a point where all his **advantages**—his **Egyptian education, his palace connections, his old ambitions**—were nothing more than **dust in the wind**.

Moses was **as good as dead**.

And that's the point.

Because when Moses **encounters YHWH**, he does so as a **dead man**—in the very place where the **Law** will later be given.

It's a profound **inclusio**—a **bookend**, where the thing **culminates where it begins**.

The Call of the Old and Broken

Moses isn't the **only one** in this pattern.

Take **Abraham**—a **miserable, childless, mostly dead** man living a **meager** existence in a **land he doesn't even want**.

He's **restless**, aching for **meaning** and **fulfillment**, almost to the point of **desperation**. But he's **old**, and he has **no heir**. Life has dealt him a **bad hand**.

And yet—**YHWH reveals Himself** not to the **young**, the **strong**, the **capable**—but to the ones who are **past their prime**.

The ones who are **tired**.

The ones who **have nothing left**.

And somehow, these **late years** become their **best years**.
It's a **divine paradox**.
And the hearers will note:
The **cultural idols of youth** are **nowhere** to be found.
The **founders** of their faith were **not men who had it all together**—they were men who had been **completely emptied**.
Moses and Abraham brought **absolutely nothing** to **God**.
That's why He could **move so powerfully** through them.

Get Out of the Way

This is **YHWH's message** to the hearers throughout history:

> *Can you please stop trying to deviate from My plan as if your ideas are helpful?*
> *You're kind of getting in My way.*
> *If you trust My plan, I'll be able to do incredible things.*
> *Surrender your ways of knowing.*
> *Don't trust in what others consider strength.*

The Final Revival?

Considering the **theme of inclusio** throughout **Salvation History**, I can't help but wonder:
What if the **great end-times revival** will look like the **first revivals**?
What if, instead of the **youth-driven movements** we keep looking for (*and let's be clear—there are many wonderful things about youth*), the **real revival** is coming through those with an **old heart**?
A heart that has **stopped trying** to **conjure revival**.

Because **revival** today is often treated like a **recipe**—something cooked in a **liturgical kitchen**:

- **Pray.**
- **Wait on God.**
- **Worship for extended periods.**
- **Stir up the prophetic.**
- **Fast.**

And don't get me wrong—**these are all good things**.
But if we're being honest?
I just described **monastic life**.
And let's be clear:
Nobody fasts and prays **better** than a **Franciscan friar**.
Jesus came drinking and eating.
John came fasting.
Which one is the **recipe for revival**?
Surely, there is a **time for both**—a time for **remembrance and acts of gluttony**, and a time for **remembrance and acts of restraint**.
Human effort is **commendable**.
But I'm not looking for an **aesthetic Pentecostal ascent** by **college students with no job**, holding up their **zeal as a sign** of the last great move of God.
If **history is bookended**, I'm looking at the **old guys**—the ones who **traverse the faithful paths**.
The **boring** paths.
The ones who **do the hard yards** of **life, ministry, and faithfulness**.

Revival, Babel, and the Protestant Work Ethic

Church **building** and **revival culture**?
 Sometimes, it feels a **little too much like Babel**.
 Like we're constructing **monuments to ourselves**, shaped by:

- The **Protestant work ethic**,
- **Western individuality**,
- **Corporate metrics** for what **growth and health** should look like,
- And what *seems right to a man* in **this cultural moment**.

Let's take one example.

The Absurdity of Metaverse Church

Let's talk about the **Metaverse**—where people put on **VR headsets**, sit in a **virtual sanctuary**, and listen to an **avatar preacher** deliver a **digitized sermon**.
 I heard someone defend it:

 "I'll go anywhere people are."

 Cool. That's great. You're an **evangelist**.
 But that **isn't** a **church**.
 Also, can we just agree that every idea we had in 2021 was utterly moronic?

Online Church Isn't Church. Sorry.

The **Church** is where people are gathered in **physical proximity** to one another.

It has **geography**.

We are **not** Gnostics. We are **not** Neo-Platonists with a **low view** of **bodies and places**.

I know a **young pastor** who has aggressively **decentralized his church** in favor of **online gatherings and digital equipping**.

And I get it—he's **an evangelist**.

But his **ecclesiology is warped**.

Because **bodies and places matter to God**.

And God still meets people **in places**.

How the Reformers Defined Church

When the **Reformers** were trying to figure out **life after Roman Catholicism**, they had to answer a crucial question:

What constitutes a church?

They landed on a simple definition:

"Where the sacraments are administered and the Gospel is preached faithfully."

That's a **good** starting point.

The Importance of Sacraments and Right Preaching

I like the idea of **sacraments being administered**—which, by the way, requires a **teaching elder** overseeing the **administration**.

Translation?

- I don't get to **stay home** and administer **communion to myself.**
- It **demands physical proximity**—a place, a people.
- More importantly, it demands **right standing in a community of faith.**

And I like the idea that a **church is a place where the Gospel is preached faithfully**—meaning:

- A **church** is **not** a place where **heresy abounds**.

The **Reformers** were saying:

We are sacramental—we believe that Christ shows up uniquely in the gathering of the saints.

This **Real Presence of Christ**, manifesting **corporately**, is what **differentiates** a **church gathering** from:

- Sitting **at home** with no spiritual authority,
- A **pub meetup**,
- Some guy **strumming a harp and whistling a hymn**.

God Shows Up—In Places He's Wanted

Yes, God can show up **anywhere**.

But the presence of God for the **purpose** of **dispensing supernatural grace** in the Christian life?

That **hits differently** in the gathered church.

Under the **supervision of faithful elders**—those who have given their **lives** to **creating a prophetic environment**—the **Spirit mediates and manifests** the **presence of Christ**.

Revival and the Glory of God

Let's take a quick historical **survey** of how Christians have created environments for **God to show up**.

And by the way, **He shows up**.

He **turns up** where He is **wanted**.

Yes, **God is omnipresent**.
But His **glory**?
His **manifest presence**?
That shows up **uniquely**.

"I don't worship to get more of God. I worship because I have the indwelling Spirit."

Yeah, that's **not** what James suggests in **James 4**.
And don't confuse the **Spirit of Adoption** with **Spirit Birth**.
Paul says, **"Be filled with all the fullness of God."**
There's a **fullness, bonehead**.
There's always **more** of God.
There's **one baptism** but **many fillings**.

The Real Presence and the Traditions That Pursue It

The **Catholics** taught the **Real Presence**, and honestly, they did well.
They say:

"You want the Presence of God? Come and receive it by faith at Mass. And as you do this by faith, you will receive super-ordinary grace to live the Christian life. Jesus wants to make Himself known to you, and He does this through the Eucharist."

And I'm **a fan** of the **Table of the Lord**.
I **totally** believe that **Jesus manifests Himself** in this way.
The **Protestants** kept the **Eucharist**—and this **high** or sacra-mental idea of the **Real Presence**—but added:

"When we preach the Scriptures faithfully, Christ manifests Himself powerfully in our services."

They put more **oomph** on the **Bible** because of the **abuses of the Church**.

And I'm **a fan** of **faithful preaching**.

I **totally** believe that *"Scripture is the primary way of gazing upon Christ,"* as **John Piper** so eloquently put it.

The **Mennonites**, **Quakers**, and **Anabaptists** placed an emphasis on **contemplative prayer** and **supplication**, suggesting that the **indwelling Spirit of God** manifests Himself through the **participation of the congregation** in **waiting on God** and **silence**.

And I certainly **believe** that **God shows up** to those who **wait for Him**.

The **Pentecostals** placed a **lower** emphasis on the **Table of the Lord** and instead **focused on Spirit-manifestations** in their **prayer** or **tarrying meetings**.

They would:

- **Wait on the Lord** in **worship and prayer**,
- Practice a **1 Corinthians 14** liturgy,
- Witness **tongues, interpretation of tongues, prophecies**,
- Experience **signs and wonders** (healings, words of knowledge, personal prophecies).

All of this, they believed, was the **manifest presence of Christ** as **mediated by the Holy Spirit**.

And you know what?

I'm **fine** with that.

I **concede** that the Spirit indeed **gives evidence of Himself** through **signs and wonders** and the **building up of the Body of Christ** through **various charisms**.

The Worship Liturgy of the Late Pentecostals

Then came the **Latter Rain** and **Plains Revival Charismatic types**.

They placed **a heavy emphasis** on **musical praise and worship**, specifically **Davidic expressions of worship**:

- **Clapping**
- **Dancing**
- **Singing**
- **Shouting**
- **Lifting of the hands**
- **Psalms, hymns, spiritual songs**
- **Prophetic or spontaneous songs**

These **late Pentecostals**, already practicing **Pentecostal liturgies**, began to **study the Bible** and concluded:

> *"The liturgy needs to emphasize the Psalms and the tabernacle expressions of David."*

And I'm **so into this**.
I am **convinced** that **God shows up when I praise Him**.
In fact, I think this **liturgy** clearly **connects both Testaments**.

Why This Matters

That's a **brief sketch** of some of these church traditions.

All of them, in their **own way**, were **trying to do the same thing**:

> *Create an atmosphere where Jesus Christ is 'among us' and we sense His work.*

Now, let me be clear.

I'm **not** writing this book to tell anybody **exactly** what **portions** of these traditions they ought to incorporate.

But I **am** saying this:

I **honor** these traditions.

Because they are **blatantly about the Presence of Jesus Christ**, as **mediated by the Spirit**.

And they were **asking the right question**—because they understood **why the Church exists**.

Evangelicalism: Its Strengths and Its Faults

Now, my **concern** about **Evangelicalism** begins with **the name**—and ends with **its influence**.

Evangelicalism could be summarized as:

> *A movement in the American Christian tradition where, in response to the backsliding of mainline denominationalism, biblically based leaders began to take a stand.*

Rightly concerned that a **once-Godly country** was falling into **unchecked Secularism**, leaders like **Billy Graham emerged** as

winsome, biblical cultural evangelists calling backsliders **back to God**.

This movement was marked by:

- **Gospel fidelity**,
- **Outreach**,
- **A clear call to repentance**.

Evangelism to **Americans** is the **main thrust** of **Evangelicalism**. Which means its **first** question is not,

"How do we get God in the building?"

but rather,

"How do we get Americans in the building?"

And look—I don't have a **problem** with **Evangelism**.

In fact, we **desperately need it**.

Without **Evangelists**, the **Body of Christ** is missing an **important Ascension Gift**.

Jesus **Himself** personally **gifted** the **Church** with **Evangelists**— and we need **more** of them.

The Role of Evangelists in the Church

But if an **Evangelist** is going to **run a church** (*and let's be clear— there are some truly great Evangelists who lead churches well*), they have to **prioritize why a church exists**.

I know—I sound like a **broken record**.

But let me say it **again**:

The Church exists to:

1. **Worship God**
2. **Equip the Saints**
3. **Reach the World**

In that order.

Sunday Mornings: 2/3 for God and the Church

So what does that mean for **Sunday mornings**?

They are **primarily** (*if we're just cutting the math that way*) **two-thirds for God and the Saints**.

And honestly?

I don't even think it's meant to be **cut that way**.

The Early Church's Priorities

When we read **Acts 2**, we see the **Church prioritizing**:

- **Presence**
- **Equipping**

And then what happens?

God adds to their number.

Because if we just look at the **Ascension Gifts** in **Ephesians 4**, Evangelism is **one-fifth** of the **leadership gifts**.

The Obsession with Numbers

Now, let me be **direct**.

It **feels** like the focus for **many pastors** today is:

- **Decisions.**
- **Baptisms.**

And **pardon me** for sounding **cynical**—but I'm a **critic** because I **love** and **appreciate** the Church.

And quite **frankly**?

These numbers get inflated.

Why?

Because that's the **metric**.

That's the **bragging right**.

And honestly?

We've got some **fibbers**.

The Problem with Presence-Driven Metrics

Here's the thing about **Presence**—

It isn't **quantifiable**.

It **doesn't** get you a **speaking gig**.

It **doesn't** land you a **bigger book advance**.

You **can't** wear it as a **badge**.

But for **1,500 years**—that was the **entire** focus of the **Church**.

Now?

We have pastors talking about their **numbers**.

Numbers Matter—But They Aren't Everything

Now, let's be fair.

I'm **not** going to **despair**.

And I'm **not** one of those people who **doesn't care** about numbers.

Numbers **matter** to God.

We see it **clearly** in **Acts 3**:

Three thousand were added to the Church.
The **Bible counts**.
I have **no problem counting**.
But let's bring it back to the **context** you and I are in:

The Influence of the Seeker-Sensitive Movement.

The **Seeker-Sensitive Movement** didn't just **change** how Evangelicals **carpet the auditorium**.
It **influenced** Pentecostals and Charismatics.
And **to some degree**—I suppose I'm **appreciative**.
It forced **many of us** to **reconsider** how:

- **Efficient** (*ugh, such a cringe word when you're Presence-driven*),
- **Effective** (*equally cringe*),
- Or **engaging** our **services** really were.

Or better yet—
It **made the Boomers** realize that **other people besides themselves existed**.

Making Evangelicals More Human

The **Seeker Movement** made Evangelicals **pay attention** to:

- **Millennial methods**.
- The **fact that they had children**.
- The **fact that the culture was shifting**.

It **made them younger**.
To this day, my **dad** is **way cooler** and more **personable** than he used to be.

He was **stuck in yacht-rock fever pitch**.
And then—
He **lightened up**.
(*Granted, us boys pushed him to the limit of breaking, of course.*)

A Chestertonian Reflection

What **Seeker-Sensitivity** did, for all its flaws, was make **Evangelicals more human**.
And for that?
I'm **grateful**.
G. K. Chesterton once said something along the lines of:

> *We are called to be in the world, but not of it. But some Christians aren't even in the world.*[1]

And I **agree**.
Being in the world is a good thing.
If **Beauty** is **transcendent**, Christians should **know about it**.
Christians should **know** non-Christians.
They **shouldn't** be afraid of:

- **Golf**.
- **Art**.

---

[1] "The Church could not afford to swerve a hair's breadth on some things, if she was to continue her great and daring experiment of the irregular equilibrium. Once she was asked by a sceptic what was the difference between the Christian idea and the modern idea of progress merely for the sake of progress. The Christian asked the sceptic to formulate his idea of progress. The sceptic said, 'I suppose we should move with the times.' The Christian said, 'The times are going the wrong way; the Church ought to be a check on the world, not a compromise with it. The world is what the saints corrected. I do not say the Church was worldly; I almost said it was not worldly enough.'" This is the exact quote and I am of course abbreviating and synthesizing, but the idea is Chestertonian. See chapters 2 and 7 of Orthodoxy for a wider scope on this topic.

- **Theatre** (*Pentecostals, I'm looking at you*).
- **A deck of cards** (*Put the pearls down, Carol*).

Seeker, Boomers, and the Lost Art of Liturgy

Seeker helped **Boomers** realize that they had gotten **older than God**.

But my **concern** is that it did **irreparable damage** (*in many cases*) to our **liturgies**—the **way we believe** the **presence of God** is welcomed in our gatherings—and ultimately to our already **vulnerable doctrine** of the Church.

And perhaps what irks me even more—as a **lover of the Church**—is how the **Boomer emphasis** on **Seeker-Sensitive churches** discipled the **next generation** of **Gen X and Elder Millennial leaders**.

These leaders **not only** embraced a **Seeker liturgy** as *ex cathedra* (*as if it descended from heaven itself*), but they **doubled down** on postures and platitudes that **portray ambiguity and nuance** on **essential doctrines** as some kind of **otherworldly wisdom**.

How the Seeker Model Became the Boomer Inheritance

Here's what happened:

1. **The Boomers updated the "vibe"** of church to make it **less cringey** for **unbelievers**.
2. **Their disciples built doctrine** on **Boomer methodology** instead of **Scriptural theology**.
3. **The Boomers were still theological conservatives**, trying to remove **awkward barriers** for **Joe Visitor**.

4. **Their disciples?** They **don't even know** how to spell **theology**—and **despise** taking a **position** on anything.

The Boomer Seekers avoided political affiliation—but at least admitted that abortion was a problem.

Their disciples avoid "harsh-sounding Scriptures" and feign an allyship with "Women's Rights."

I'll **not concern myself** here with the **Bermuda Triangle** of **Seeker Evangelicalism**—where the **political legacy** of their children is **lost**.

My **bone to pick** is with **what this concept has done to our liturgies**.

Or, to be more precise—

How the Seeker Movement has become a Shiloh Incident.

A Warning, Not a Prophetic Indictment

Now, I'm **not** the prophet **Jeremiah**.

And I'm **not** bringing a **prophetic indictment** against the **Seeker Movement**, declaring that it has **ruined** the **Evangelical Church in America** and that now **God is gone, never to return**.

But I **do** think our **greatest weakness** as **Evangelicals**—(*Bible-believing Christians who want to reach people for Christ, and yes, I'll include Pentecostals in this*)—is that:

Sunday mornings have ceased to be a place where the Presence of God is the focus and where discipleship takes place.

The **Church** is supposed to be a **resting place** for the **Presence of God**—where our **liturgies**—

- **Eucharist**
- **Preaching the Word faithfully**
- **Praise and Worship**

- **Manifestation of the Gifts**
- (*Or all of these combined in one service!*)

—**support encounter** with God.

The Point of Liturgy Is Encounter

The **point** of **liturgies** is **encounter**.

A **Sunday morning service** is meant to be a place where:

- **The priests minister to the Lord.**
- **Fire comes upon the altar.**

But what **Seeker creates** is **passive consumerism**.

Where acceptable offerings are not offered in the corporate gathering—and the result is a God who is faithful to not show up where He is not wanted.

If my **philosophy** is that the **Sunday morning gathering** is **primarily a place** for **liturgies to be practiced** by a **priesthood** that desires **encounter with God** (*which is what the Church confessed for centuries*), then I'm **not** going to **gloss over** our liturgies.

I'm **not** going to let the band **whip through four songs** and be **satisfied** with a church that merely **sings** or **mimics charismatic worship actions**.

Teaching the Why

I'm going to **teach the Church why:**

- We **lift our hands** (*Psalm 141:2—it's a sacrifice that pleases God*).

- We **sing praises and prayers** (*Hebrews 13:16—it's a sacrifice of praise that pleases God*).
- We **give our money** (*Hebrews 13:17—it's a sacrifice that pleases God*).
- We **take the Eucharist** as a **moment of encounter**, not **mere symbolism**.
- We **teach the Scriptures expositionally**, not just **regurgitate motivational TikTok reels**.

I'm going to explain that they aren't here to be impressed with our platform but to minister to God.

The Presence of God Must Be the Priority

However your **church** believes **Presence manifests—pursue it.**

- Don't want to do **Communion every Sunday? Cool.**
- Don't believe the **Eucharist is Sacramental? Fine.**

But **dig down deep** into whatever **tradition you have** that you **believe manifests Christ in the building.**
Give people Jesus.
Don't give them:

- A **poor man's David Goggins.**
- The **same message over and over again.**
- **Marketing gimmicks.**
- A **shallow sense of community** (*yoga classes have better community than most small groups*).

The Role of the Old Men

And every **church** will have its **emphasis**.

- I love that **Charismatic churches** dig down **deep** into **worship as encounter**.
- I love that **Baptists** dig down **deep** into **expository preaching as encounter**.

That's **Presence**.
They are **giving their people Christ**.
And many times?
It's the **old guys leading this**.
They've **rejected the innovation of youth**, the **gimmicks**, the technology—and they've **held onto the faithful paths** that create a séance with the Creator of the universe.

Seeker's Greatest Lie: "We Need to Get Out of the Four Walls"

Seeker **reversed the order** of the **Church** with its **stupid slogans**, like:

> *"We need to get out of the four walls of the Church."*

Dumb.
You spent **one two-hour service a week**—maybe **two max**—inside the Church.

The **rest** of the time you were **outside the Church**.

You didn't need to **switch the entire point** of why a **Sunday morning exists**—you just needed to **remember how to be human**.

The Future of the Church

This is my **point** about the **old men of Salvation History**—

And why I wouldn't be surprised if the **innovation of youth** in the **Church** is **bypassed** for the **simple faith of desperate men**.

Because the **Sunday morning gathering** is **primarily for Christians**—to be **continually shaped by their worship and their God**.

And as the **Presence of God grows thick**, unbelievers who are **invited**—or rather, **drawn by God Himself**—will:

- **Taste and see** that the Lord is good.
- **Sense something powerful** in **worship, prayer, teaching, and fellowship**.
- Witness the **Spirit animating the Church**.

But what we **cannot do** is **build something unrecognizable to God**—and **lose everybody**, including **God Himself**.

Chapter Two
Where Israel Went Sideways

Jeremiah is presumably the author of *First* and *Second Kings*, a theologically motivated history of the unraveling of the United Kingdom of Israel, and then the Northern and Southern Kingdoms, respectively. His work explains to the exiled community why trouble has come upon them. In one sense, *Kings* is a theodicy—an explanation of why God has allowed, or rather, had a hand in, Israel's suffering. This community, reeling from devastating loss, is asking questions like, *Has God abandoned us? What about His promises to David and Solomon? What about the Temple?*

What was all that sweet talk?

Some scholars refer to *Kings* as a *Deuteronomistic History* because the author relies on the Mosaic book of *Deuteronomy* to help the people critique the behavior and postures of Israel and Judah's kings.

You wanna know why God got actively involved in our destruction and stirred up the Assyrians and Babylonians against us? Keep one hand in the book of Deuteronomy and one hand in this history of our kings, and tell me where you see a departure from the Law of Moses—and the warnings from YHWH about what would happen if the kings and the people violated the Law in such an indignant way.

The work of a prophet in the Old and New Testament is not limited to receiving a dream or vision and relaying that message to the people of God or their leaders. It is not limited to spontaneous, ecstatic utterances into an open mic, words of faith declared over someone at an altar, or impressions from the Spirit texted to a friend in crisis. These may be helpful expressions of prophetic ministry, but one of the oft-neglected and seldom-practiced ministries of a prophet is to:

a) Locate where on the timeline of Salvation History the people of God are; b) Understand the socio-political context in which the people of God find themselves; c) Identify biblical narratives that are not only *written for our learning* but are particularly insightful for the moment we are leading and living in.

In short, selecting narratives to instruct people is prophetic work.

And that's what Jeremiah does in the book of *Kings*.

If the exilic community is asking, *Where did we go wrong?* Jeremiah starts at the beginning of their descent into hell. The way the book is arranged is like a massive rollercoaster. If you've ever been on an insanely large rollercoaster (Canada has two of the highest ones in North America at *Canada's Wonderland* just outside Toronto), you know that big rollercoasters start with a massive, bloodcurdling drop. And that's how *1 Kings* starts.

David is dead, and Solomon takes his place. And this is gonna sound absolutely nuts to you, but Saul and Solomon form an *inclusio* around David—the man after God's own heart (who is, in fact, a dirtbag—but we love him anyway). Perhaps the idea is that a king who serves God wholeheartedly and prioritizes the words and worship of God is *rare*, while a king who relies on his own counsel and rejects the words and worship of God is *normal*.

Solomon, like Saul, starts strong.

They both have a desire to do what is right. They both show incredible humility toward God and man. They both initially have great relationships with the prophetic and priestly community. But they both die *idolators* and *traitors* to YHWH.

Solomon has an especially good start. He asks God for wisdom. He writes Scripture. He obviously has a touch of God on him—so much so that not only are his writings memorialized through divine inspiration, but his wisdom brings him a level of *glory and fame* that is second to none in human history. His learned mouth drips with otherworldly sagacity.

God clearly answers Solomon's request for wisdom. So what gives? He's rich beyond our wildest dreams. He's allied with the baddest dudes. His armies, horses, chariots, and mercenaries are uncountable. Everyone wants to be his friend. Israel has the most territory, the most gold, the most safety, the most peace, and the biggest economic boom in its history.

Surely our problems don't begin with Solomon, Jeremiah?

But the *click-click-click* of the rollercoaster's slow ascent to terrifying heights starts in *1 Kings 7*, where the narrative turns. Solomon takes a **thirteen-year hiatus** from constructing the Temple of God to focus on his own mansion and a grand house for his foreign wife.

As we read further along in *1 Kings 7*, after this shift in priorities, the author continues his critiques of Solomon—problems we weren't previously aware existed.

Now immediately, we contrast Solomon's priorities with David's priorities, because that's what the author of *Kings* is constantly doing. In fact, David becomes the repeated epitaph on the failures and graves of Israel and Judah's kings: *They did not walk in the ways of their father David.*

A rough outline of *2 Samuel*:

a) David becomes king of Judah. b) David becomes king of all Israel. c) David builds the Tabernacle for YHWH. d) God gives David victories over his enemies. e) David makes some bad decisions.

The narrative is clear: David's priority was to bring the Ark into Jerusalem, construct a tabernacle for it, and establish a system of nonstop worship that combined Mosaic observance with Davidic revelation.

David innovated—under the inspiration of the Holy Spirit—an atmosphere of worship around the presence of God. David wasn't satisfied to let the priests have all the fun. He wanted to *minister to the Lord*, and he found a way to do so through demonstrative praise accompanied by music.

This is nowhere in the Law of Moses. David's system is totally unique. And yet, it captures the *spirit* of what YHWH desired.

I remember my dad explaining to me the *spirit* of the law versus the *letter* of the law—not in a biblical context, but in a *"This-is-the-kind-of-heart-I-want-in-you"* home context.

If my dad said, *"Lights out at 8 p.m. tonight, guys. You have an early morning,"* the **letter** of the law was 8 p.m.—I had to be in bed with the lights out. But the **spirit** of the law was, *"We need to get to bed early because we have a full day."* So if I turned the lights out at 8 p.m. but kept reading *TinTin* comics until 9 p.m. by flashlight, I had transgressed the **spirit** of the law while keeping the **letter**—and that was unacceptable to my dad.

If my dad asked me to clean the car, the **letter** of the law was, *"Make sure there's no McDonald's wrappers and empty Coke cans on the floor in the back seat."* But the **spirit** of the law was, *"Take a cloth and some disinfectant and give it a solid wipe. Maybe buy an air freshener, too, you filthy pagan."* And the reason I'd go the extra mile for my dad? Because I loved him and wanted to please him.

The **letter** of the law: *"Never show up empty-handed to a party."* The **spirit** of the law: *"Never bring a bottle of wine you wouldn't drink—bring that Camus!"*

The **letter** of the law: *"Buy the person you love a birthday present."* The **spirit** of the law: *"I bought them the latest PlayStation, and they're going to lose their minds at how extravagant this is!"*

David knew the **letter** but lived the **spirit**.

His approach to God: *How extravagant can I get?*

This was David's kingly priority—put God first, and do so extravagantly. He built an atmosphere of worship in Israel that mirrored the one he created in the shepherd fields. Mass choirs, a roster of musicians, newly written songs and hymns, and national worship events that stirred the congregation's hearts toward YHWH Himself.

Whenever there is revival in Israel, there is a **Tabernacle of David** revival. And when the **Tabernacle of David** is abandoned, and the songs to YHWH die out, the nation backslides.

The Songs of Amos: Not the Songs of David

Let's be clear: the songs sung during Amos's prophesying were **not** the songs of David in the **Tabernacle**.

This was the **height of apostasy**—when songs were lifted, not to YHWH, but to **pagan altars and idols**. This was the **Jerusalem** of **Solomon's later years**—a city choked with **idolatry**, its skyline decorated with shrines to foreign gods.

David's practices—his **liturgies**, his **disciplines**, his **extravagant worship**—were what kept his heart **loyal** to YHWH.

And no, this doesn't mean **David didn't have catastrophes**.

He had **two massive failures**—numbering Israel and **Bathsheba**.

But take note: these **exact** sins repeat in **Solomon**—

- **Self-reliance** (numbering Israel),
- **Womanizing** (foreign wives).

David repents.
Solomon does not.

When Love Corrupts a King

1 Kings 7–8 lays it out.

Solomon's **heart** is led astray by his **foreign wives**.

This isn't about **ethnicity** or **race**—this is about **worship**. These women bring **their gods**, and they **demand Solomon join them**. And because Solomon **loves these women profoundly**, he does.

He **wants to hold their hands during the slow songs**—but the slow songs are at the **altars of Molech** and the **Baals**.

(*Reminder: Molech was the one who required child sacrifice.*)

And Solomon doesn't just **permit** this corruption—he **builds altars** to these demonic entities **in Jerusalem itself**.

The Irony of Solomon

Here's the **paradox** of Solomon:

He's the **boy genius** with all the **brains**—

And the **worst** political instincts.

His **heart** hijacks his **head**.

Sound **familiar**?

We are **living in a Solomonic Age**—

Where **wisdom abounds** (we have Scripture, the work of the Spirit, theological resources beyond our ancestors' wildest dreams)...

And yet our **hearts betray us**.

James K.A. Smith & The Power of Liturgy

James K. A. Smith speaks to this. He argues that **our liturgies shape our hearts**—both our **daily** and **corporate** practices.[2]

His point?

The habits of the heart—not the brain—are the center of human activity: you don't just think your way to holiness–you worship your way to it.

We must **guard our thoughts**, because **thoughts become practices**, and **practices become loves**.

And once something becomes a **love**—

It's too late.

You think, **you do, you love.**

How Love is Formed: The Gym, Carnivore Diets, and Liturgy

Think about it like **going to the gym**.

At first? **I hated it.**

But I knew it was the **right** thing to do. So I created a **routine**.

At first, I **hated** it.

Then I made **friends** there.

Then I found a **time that worked**.

Then I **pressed through**.

Eventually?

It became something I **loved**.

Same thing with my **carnivore diet**.

I'm **40 days in.**

---

[2] This book is absolutely wild, perhaps one of the greatest theological resources on the human soul and the power of liturgies. If you haven't read *You Are What You Love: The Spiritual Power of Habit* (2016), well, you're asleep at the wheel. Awake, O Sleeper. Read this book!

It's **awful**.

I feel **gross**.

I'm waiting for all that **"mental clarity"** and **"energy"** to kick in.

I **miss cold champagne**.

But I **cringe** at the idea of eating what I used to.

Now?

I **love grass-fed steak**.

I **love the taste**.

I **love the practice** of carnivore.

I **love** that I finally fit into my clothes for the first time in **two years**.

Becoming the Liturgy

Smith's argument?

Liturgy shapes our loves.

Thinking right is great—but it has to become practice in order to shape the heart.

This is the **whole point** of **corporate worship**:

We **sing the liturgy** until we **become the liturgy**.

You ever been in church, singing some **emotional song** about **loving God**, and immediately think:

"I don't love God this much—I'm a fraud."

Yeah. That's normal.

But in the **liturgical tradition**, that's **not inauthentic**.

It's **expected**.

We **sing** what we **aspire** to.

We **declare** what we **long to believe**.

Until?

The **Word becomes flesh** in us.

Until our **hearts catch up** to the words on our lips.

Until we can say, **"God, I really love you! This has become true, and You have accomplished this in me!"**

I don't **sing praise** because I feel it.

I don't **sing praise** because I *am* it.

I **sing praise** because my **flesh cries out** for the **Living God**.

The Click-Click-Click of Solomon's Doom

The first **click-click-click** of the rollercoaster—**"How We Lost the Presence of God and Why He Destroyed Us"**—

Was the **liturgies of Solomon**.

His **practices** corrupted his **heart**.

His **heart** corrupted his **brain**.

And even a **brain gifted by God** can't sustain that.

The Protestant Church's Liturgy Crisis

This is why we need to **reconsider** our **Protestant liturgies**.

Right now?

The Shepherd hasn't returned to the ninety-nine.

He's gone to Love Island with the Prodigal Son and hasn't been seen in decades.

Our people **don't have opportunities** to **practice the liturgy**.

Our people **aren't trained in it**.

And the **average Evangelical church**?

Copy-pasted Charismatic worship without discipling their congregation in it.

People lift their hands for the same reason English **football fans** lift their hands:

Mimesis.

The Lost Congregation

People think they **give** to a church.

People think **praise** is **optional**.

People think **church** is about **inspiration**—finding their **dreams** and being **happy**.

And because we are **ashamed** of the **Presence practices** Seekers don't understand, we don't just **hurry them**—

We almost despise them.

And the **result**?

A **congregation out of habit**.

A **congregation out of love**.

A **congregation whose brains are hijacked by their hearts**— and hearts will *always* find something to love.

They may **keep showing up**—for now.

But soon?

They start **building their own house** instead of **building God's house**.

And then?

They start constructing **altars to idols**—which eventually **lead them into bondage**.

The Great Driver of Deconstruction

This is **one of the major drivers** of **Deconstruction**:

Because my church never explained liturgy to me, my heart has been a Desperado—looking for many things to love.

And I go and **find them**.

But the **Christian corruption** of these **other loves**?

Far worse.

The Gym Doesn't Dumb Itself Down—So Why Do We?

"We gotta stop talking Christianese—people won't understand."
Bro.
Nobody at the **gym** stops using **gym talk.**
Nobody **hides the fit people.**
My trainer is a **genius.** I have to **ask her to explain things.**
But I **know my condition**—so I **lean in.**
Solomon the Wise Becomes Solomon the Fool
Solomon **the wise** becomes **Solomon the dummy**—
Because his **brain** gets **hijacked by his heart.**
And Jeremiah's hearers?
Stunned.
Wait…
Solomon is the guy who messed this whole thing up?
Rich boy with all the wisdom from God?
Yep.
*Smarty-pants with the **Scrooge McDuck vault of gold coins**?*
Absolutely.
He was the **smartest dumbest king** because he thought he could **innovate** his way out of the **liturgies of his father.** He assumed that his **brain** would protect his **heart.**

But, as my dear friend **Ken Malmin** once said:

> *"The heart is best protected when it is given."*

And Solomon?
He **did not give** his heart through **liturgies to the Lord.**

Corporate Worship: The Bedrock of Liturgy

Our **corporate worship services** form the **foundation** of our training in **liturgies**.

This is where **leadership exterior** to our **will** sets the **pace for us**.

That's the **beauty of it**.

It's training.

And training hurts–sucks, even.

A Sunday Morning Call to Worship Should Sound Like This:

"Church, we are praising God the way the Bible says for the next 25 minutes. Lift your hands. Crucify your Canadian flesh that hates being told what to do and obey God. Crucify your Canadian flesh that doesn't like making any noise in public, that resents people who are loud anywhere at any time. Lift your voice to the Lord. Shout to God with a voice of triumph. Declare His praises aloud. Obey the Bible. Don't be conformed to the cultural pattern of Canada—be transformed by the renewing of your mind through Scripture."

Zero **safety**.

Total **beatdown by the trainer**.

The **new guy** can **handle the heat**.

He needs **God**.

He **wants** God.

He is **eager** to learn the **lingo**.

He will have **questions later**—they can be answered.

Let him **squirm**.

God is working.

And **church** is **not about him**.

It's about **God** and the **Saints** before it's about **him**.

Tithes & Offering: A Call to Worship

"Church, we are continuing our worship through our giv-ing. At this church, we return to the Lord ten percent of the 100 percent He has given us. He has given us the power to get wealth. If you have breath in your lungs, it's because of Him. In Him, we live and move and have our being. And because of this, we are thankful."

*"We are not only thankful to be alive—we are thankful to have our names written in the Lamb's Book of Life. We are thankful to be a part of the Body of Christ—evidence of God's saving work. When God saves us, He adds us to the Church. And so we give thanks by offering our money as a sacrifice to God—our money represents our blood, sweat, and tears. Our **glory, our dialed-in-ness, our spark, our long, hard hours of toil.** And by giving it to the Lord, we are offering Him our **lives** back."*

*"Yes, this money will be used for the Kingdom of God, and the Church is the primary vehicle for the expansion of the Kingdom. But don't lose sight: you are giving to Jesus Christ today. When it leaves your hands, it goes into His. This is wor-ship. **Worship God!**"*

Hit them with the **hard stuff**.
Don't **shy away** from it.
Drill down.
Disciple them.
Let them **practice** the liturgy of **turning their back on the love of money.**
God shows up when they do this.
Don't **rob them** of **Presence.**

Preaching the Word: A Call to Attention

"Church, we are reading the Bible today in our sermon. The Bible is God's Word. If you need a word from God today, good news: every time we read the Scriptures, the Holy Spirit speaks."

"We put a high value on reading the Scriptures because they accomplish something in us and through us that my insights and killer jokes cannot."

"Lean into the Word this morning. Get your notebook out. Write down what the Lord is saying. Prepare your heart for the Scriptures. Ask God to remove the scales of deception and spiritual blindness. Ask the Lord to change your mind today—to help you repent—as you hear the Word."

"God is gonna show up as we discuss these things."

Don't Rob the People of the Word of God

Yes, you should be **hilarious**.
Yes, humor is a **language** that helps to explain **truth**.
But make sure that the **Bible** is the focus.
Not some **leadership platitude** or **empty aphorism**.

Altar Calls, Ministry Time & Communion

*"If you need prayer today, we have a team waiting for you. Come to the altar and believe God for a breakthrough. We believe in the power of prayer—that God hears us when two or three agree on earth. **Come now!**"*

Encourage people to **receive ministry**.
Let them **sense** that **God is here in the room**.
Because He is.

Communion: A Call to Faith

If you do **Communion, explain** it.

And add a **faith element**—

That the **presence of Christ is really here** to **work** and **move in power.**

> *"This isn't a mid-service snack. It's not just a time to reflect on Christ's death. It's the cup of blessing—we are eating and drinking grace into our lives, if we do so by faith."*
>
> *"You need healing? Believe for it now. Receive the blood of Christ. **By His stripes, we are healed.**"*
>
> *"You need power to live the victorious Christian life? Eat now—His body was broken for you, that you would be healed and whole. You participate in His very life now."*

Let Church Be Church

Prophesy over someone.

Pause the service and pray for someone.

Sing a bridge one more time.

Sense what **God is doing.**

He is **present.**

Teach them how to **do the liturgy** so that they may **become the liturgy.**

Teach them how to **give their heart.**

And explain that when they do **all of this**—

The **Glory of God comes upon the Church.**

Yes, I Know...

Our **kids' volunteers** are **overrun.**

It's **Lord of the Flies** back there.
They've got **Piggy on a spit**.
I **get it**—
You have **16,000 people** and you're running **eight services**.
Time constraints are **real**.
Fine.
But maybe it's **time** to add five more minutes to the **clock**.
Or maybe it's **time** to **trim some fat**—
Maybe the **transitions are too long**.
Maybe that **first praise song** can **go**, since it means **absolutely nothing**, and you haven't discipled your people into **dancing** yet anyway.

Catholics & The Weirdness of Mass

If the **Catholics** can camp out on the **Eucharist for Presence** and still get **Mass done in an hour**—
Maybe we can **rethink some things**.
There is **nothing stranger** than **Mass**.
And I **love that for them**.

Young People Are Running to the Catholic Church & The Gym

You ever try to become **Catholic?**
Good luck.
Hilariously, young people are **flocking** to the Catholic Church **the same way** they seem to gather en masse at **gyms**. It's kind of annoying, actually. How can you afford a membership at LifeTime? I'm sick of waiting 45 minutes for the bench press only to be laughed at because I'm weak and old and sad.
But **Why?**

Because they are **hungry to learn**.

May our **liturgies punch us in the gut**.

May they **change our hearts**.

May they **capture our imagination**.

And may our **rival visions of human flourishing** be **diminished**—

As we are **boldly invited** into the **vision** and **practices** of the Church.

Chapter Three

The Babel Church

In Rome—particularly around the Colosseum and Trevi Fountain—there are an infinitude of persistent-to-the-point-of-pain street merchants, typically from Africa or Pakistan, attempting to sell junk to tourists.

Keychains. Glow-in-the-dark spinners. Neon helicopters. Bracelets.

Most of it? Absolute **trash**.

Some of them actually have skills. Some can paint or sketch you on the spot with surprising accuracy, drawing a small crowd as they work with a charcoal stick and a cigarette hanging from their lips like they stepped out of an Italian arthouse film. But generally? It's overpriced gimmicky garbage straight from a Cracker Jack box.

And here's the thing:

They *know* they're selling junk nobody wants—so they have to get aggressive.

They pull on your arms. They step in your way. They demand conversations about your shoes.

The bracelet peddlers are the **worst**.

They slap a bracelet on you like an overeager carnival barker and act like it was a mutual decision. When you take it off, they go full Oscar-winning performance, clutching their chest in betrayal, claiming you *broke* it. They follow you around, screaming bloody murder about how you owe them *at least* five euros for damages, all while you're just trying to eat your gelato in peace.

Or they launch into a guilt monologue—how you wore it for a grand total of three seconds, which legally makes it yours, and now you *must* compensate them for this deep emotional injury.

Desperate?

Yeah.

And I feel for a working man just trying to survive. I do. The world isn't kind, and everyone's gotta hustle. But there's a difference between honest selling and manipulation.

And that's the point.

Forcing something on someone... pretending they want it... manufacturing guilt... demanding a transaction?

That's a scam.

The Chocolate Almond Hustle

I'll be the first to admit—

I did this exact thing as a kid.

Every year, from the time I was five until well into my middle-school years, I found myself selling chocolate almonds to raise money for my baseball team, my school, my *somebody's* fundraiser. And I was *ruthless*.

I would annoy the neighbors, harass churchgoers, set up shop outside of grocery stores, weaponizing my puppy-dog eyes and youthful innocence. If you made the mistake of making eye contact with me? Game over. You were leaving with a box of chalky, overpriced candy and I was pocketing the commission.

And most people?

They lovingly allowed themselves to be deceived—like Isaac pretending not to notice that his lamb dinner was actually mutton in disguise.

They weren't buying the candy because they *wanted* it. They were buying it because they remembered being that kid. Because they had once stood on a stranger's doorstep, shivering in the cold, clutching a box of stale fundraising goods, and had been met with either kindness or cruelty.

And so they returned the favor.

Why Do We Buy?

There's a reason we purchase stuff we don't want or need from kids.

We've been there. We know the existential terror of ringing a doorbell, wondering if some cranky adult is about to unleash their rage upon you for the audacity of offering them mid-tier chocolate in exchange for their hard-earned money.

And we love to pay it forward.

I remember the generous stranger who gave me twenty bucks and bought ten chocolate bars.

Or the guy who handed me a ten-spot and took only one, letting me devour four on the way home (because self-control is a myth when you're eight and alone with candy).

We *love* opportunities to be generous—

To feel like we're doing a small good in a world that often feels overwhelmingly bad.

Alms, Mercy & The Grace of God

And that's exactly how we *should* feel when we are pressed by those on the margins.

When the homeless ask for money, should we dismiss them because they'll *just* spend it on booze?

I don't know—maybe.

But isn't that what we *all* do with the grace of God?

Maybe giving alms isn't really about them—it's about *you*.

Maybe your soul needs to be reacquainted with how God watches *you* **waste His mercy** again and again—handing you the same forgiveness, the same second chances, the same fresh start *every single morning,* knowing full well you'll likely squander it on the same old sins.

Because mercy?

It isn't about *deserving.* It's about *becoming self-aware.*

It's a kind of high-IQ spiritual self-consciousness.

And God?

He is so much more merciful than you or I can comprehend.

> *"The Lord is compassionate and gracious,*
> *slow to anger, abounding in love."*
> —Psalm 103:8

The Manipulation Threshold

But there is a threshold in mercy—

A line between generosity and gullibility.

A point where compassion curdles into manipulation.

And let's be honest.

We're all guilty of it.

Maybe not in the full-throttle, street-merchant, arm-grabbing, bracelet-hustling way.

But in our relationships. Our jobs. Our churches.

How often do we guilt people into things?

How often do we leverage "I did this for you, so now you owe me" theology?

How often do we wrap our selfish desires in noble packaging—convincing ourselves that we're just "helping" when we're really just maneuvering people toward the outcome *we* want?

God?

He sees right through it.
And He wants to deliver us from it.
Because a life built on manipulation—
Is just another Babel waiting to collapse.

Babel: The Ultimate Scam

The Tower of Babel is exactly this kind of manipulation—
But on a systemic, global scale.
The people gather.
They settle in the land of Shinar.
They collaborate.
They scheme.
They decide:

> *"If we build this incredible tower (assumption) to where God is (assumption), then He will come down our tower (assumption) and hang out in our temple (assumption), and He will like all the fruit we give Him (assumption), and then He will have to do what we want (BIG assumption)."*

It's theology by way of **The Secret**—manifesting your way to God's favor.

Babel is **spiritual manipulation**, the ultimate act of cosmic hustle. It's a **pyramid scheme**—and not even a good one, just **a literal one**. And the punchline?

They don't even know how to build properly.
The text mocks them—

> *"These idiots used bricks instead of stone."*

That's an ancient insult. That's the biblical equivalent of an architecture professor roasting your Lego tower for poor structural integrity.

Because structures that last—the pyramids, Greek temples, the Colosseum—were built with **quarried stone**. They were built by people who knew the difference between something that could withstand the test of time and something you slap together in a weekend before it crumbles like a Jenga tower at a six-year-old's birthday party.

These guys?

They're stacking **garbage**.

It's **cheap, trendy, disposable faith**—

Faddish nonsense with a shelf life shorter than a TikTok trend.

And **fads die fast**.

The Babel of the Internet Age

And here's the craziest thing about Babel:

It's happening again.

Only now?

It's **digital**.

The internet is **our modern migration to Shinar**.

It's a **mass gathering of people with no spiritual home**, a collection of restless wanderers stitching together meaning from Reddit threads, Instagram infographics, and YouTube algorithms that keep serving them new existential crises to binge.

It's the **fastest way to spread a religious scam**.

Think about it:

Every day, people wake up and get plugged into a digital **Tower of Babel 2.0**, where all the most confused people get together and create new, experimental belief systems **on the fly**—like a theological version of Mad Libs.

The Power of Idiots in Large Groups

One of Babel's meta-lessons?
Beware **the power of idiots in large groups**.
And we're watching this in real-time.
Social media is **Babel 2.0**—a global forum where people craft personal belief systems in real time, molding their worldview based on whatever trend is most likely to get them retweets, upvotes, and heart-reacts.
It's an **ideological buffet**—except everyone's going up to the sneeze-guarded line and inventing new dishes on the spot.
Teenagers unite in a multiplicity of oddities:

- **Furry fandom.**
- **Gender invention.**
- **Bisexuality as an entry-level identity (cue "Everyone Has AIDS" from Team America).**
- **Victimhood as a lifestyle.**

(I recently read about a woman who **blinded herself with lighter fluid** because she identified as visually impaired. Welcome to the age where self-inflicted disability is considered brave, and common sense is considered a hate crime.)
The idiocy **compounds**.
And like Babel?
It gains momentum **fast**.
It's a **blitzkrieg** of chaos.
And our pastors and leaders?
They underestimate the **speed** at which **foolishness metastasizes**.
The tower takes shape.

Christian Pagans: Babel's Children

And here's the bewildering reality:

These aren't atheists.

They're **spiritual**.

They're **pagans**.

But they're not **traditional** pagans—

Not the cool kind, like Vikings who drank mead, plundered villages, and named their kids things like Ulfberht.

No—

They're **Christian Pagans**.

The Birth of Christian Paganism

Christian Pagans are **spiritualists**—

But their **morality is deeply shaped by Christianity**.

Every moral instinct they have?

It's **a product of the Christian culture they were born into**.

The Vikings?

They believed **capricious murder was a virtue**.

The Christian Pagan?

They believe **capricious murder is a vice**—

But will still contort their logic to justify **killing their unborn child** in the name of "choice."

The Christian Pagan's Conflicted Ethics

- **Every virtue they hold? Christian.**
- **Every vice they fight? Christian heresy.**

The Christian Pagan builds their worldview with **selective morality**, a **remixed version of Christianity** that aligns with their **personal preferences** but maintains a **veneer of spirituality**.

- Christian virtue: **Love. Kindness. Fairness. Equality.**
- Christian heresy: **Love with no truth. Kindness at the expense of reality. Fairness by punishing the strong. Equality through oppression.**

The closest thing they have to **true paganism**?
Abortion.
But even then?
They exonerate themselves by refusing to ask the question—
"When does life begin?"
The **god of this world has blinded their eyes**—
Or at least their moral reasoning.
God comes down from the heavens—His dwelling place—
To see what they've built.
And this, for the original audience, is an exegetical Easter egg—
Because from the very beginning, **the tower has failed**.
They never reached Him.
He had to come down.
And what He sees?
Disgusting.
Not just because of their **brazen craftiness**—
But because of their **total lack of self-awareness**.
They have forgotten:

- **Their mortality and God's immortality.**
- **Their dependence and God's independence.**
- **Their finiteness and God's infiniteness.**
- **Their need and God's all-sufficient supply.**

So what does God do?

He **rejects** the Tower of Babel.

And in a **judgment dripping with irony**—

He **confuses them**.

They sought power in unity—

He destroys them with **division**.

They wanted one tongue, one people, one movement—

He shatters them into **incoherence**.

And this?

This is Paul's **entire premise** in Romans 1.

God **gives them over to confusion**—

Because **confusion was their goal all along**.

The Babel builders thought they were **manifesting their own destiny**—

What they actually got?

A divine **unsubscribe** from God Himself.

God Rejects the Youth of the World

The youth of the world—

Its bragging point, its best bet, its greatest hope—

Blocked.

And in one of the great reversals of history—

God chooses to work with an old man.

This is the beginning of salvation history.

This is the foundation of what will become the Church—

The *ekklesia*.

The called-out ones.

And He doesn't do it by harnessing the energy of the bright-eyed, passionate, idealistic young people who are always convinced they are about to change the world with their hashtags and their ethically sourced kombucha.

Nope.

When God decides to create a people of His own, He doesn't work within the existing system.

He doesn't partner with the trending political movements.

He doesn't tap into the greatest minds of the age, or the youth with their tech startups and their ability to turn emotional outbursts into policy changes.

He rejects *everyone alive.*

And chooses *one* man.

Abram.

The Man Who Shouldn't Have Been Chosen

Abram is 75 years old.

He's *basically dead.*

He lives in the middle of nowhere, in a cultural backwater.

He has no real prospects.

His LinkedIn page would be cringe.

His best years are behind him.

His aspirations are memories.

His anxieties are many (and they only increase with age).

He has no reason to leave home—

Because at his age, leaving home isn't just difficult—

It's *suicide.*

But YHWH graciously appears to Abram.

Because YHWH knows—

That in Abram, He will find a willing heart at the end of its rope.

And that's what God does.

He doesn't show up to the slick, young, idealistic world-changers building the latest and greatest version of Babel.

He doesn't call the ones with fire in their belly and the ability to capture an audience with their passion.

He calls the one who has *nothing left* except trust in *Him.*

The one who knows he is too old, too irrelevant, too out-of-step to do anything meaningful on his own.

Abram, who should be collecting Social Security and drinking prune juice, is about to become the father of faith.

Reverse Mentoring & The Babel Church

None of this is new or surprising.

Most of us already agree:

The world is confused—and growing more so.

The Great Falling Away is both cyclical and accelerating.

But here's my thesis:

The Western Church has been so profoundly shaped by the dogmas of culture—its secular remedies for social maladies—that in some ways, it is beginning to resemble a Babel Church.

It is constructing trendy platforms—made of garbage material—

And encouraging others in their personal Babel projects—

All in an effort to reach culture and *please* God.

It wants to be relevant.

It wants to be seen as "on the right side of history."

It wants to be invited to the cool parties.

It wants to be spoken well of by *The New York Times.*

But God does not build with Babel bricks.

He does not build with trends.

He does not build with whatever ideology is currently considered enlightened.

He builds with faith.

And faith, it turns out, is found in the most unexpected places.

The Age of the Psychological Man

We live in the age of the *Psychological Man.*
A person whose entire concept of self is determined by:

- How they feel.
- How they interpret their experiences.

Or, as my friend David Kuwabara says:

"They have emoted themselves into being."

And the logical next step?
Any external criticism—that produces a *negative* emotion—
Is now irreparably injurious.
Thus, truth becomes violence.
Reality becomes oppressive.
And Christian orthodoxy?
A hate crime.

The War on Free Speech: A Spiritual Battle

Enter the war on free speech.
And Christian Conservatives already know:
This isn't just a peripheral culture war—about creating a free society.
This is a *spiritual battle*—for the nature of existence itself.
Because this?
This is why the Empire persecuted Christianity in the first place.
Because Christianity violated the pagan right to *feel good* existentially.

KILLER CHURCH VOLUME II

Christianity was the moral conscience that rained on Rome's parade.

Just read Augustine's *City of God.*

Christians were blamed for ruining the party.

They were seen as killjoys, holding the world to a standard that the world *did not* ask for.

And the world still doesn't ask for it.

Because the world never wants to be told that what it desires is wrong.

The Woke Church: Babel Rebuilt

I define the Babel Church as the *Woke Church*:

- Never offending.
- Always placating.
- Always having conversations—never reaching conclusions.
- Baptizing departures from historic Christian orthodoxy.
- Living in paranoia that somehow, somewhere, someone has been offended.
- Reading modern political grievances into ancient Scripture.

The Babel Church buys into the secular critique of Christianity—

And believes that the Church will continue committing these *atrocities*—

Unless it submits to Secularism as its moral authority.

And thus, the Babel Church *apologizes*—for its existence.

It *grovels* before the culture.

It offers up its doctrines, its traditions, its convictions for the judgment of Twitter theologians.

It desperately *wants* to be invited back to the party.

But here's the thing.

The Apology Tour Never Ends

This is why our leaders have accepted these terms.
   Why they continue to *self-flagellate*.
   And once you join the apology tour?
   There's no canceling dates.
   The apology tour is a *brick* that Babel builders manufacture—
   To construct their pseudo-spiritual house.
   It's a way of doing *penance* for agreed-upon societal sins—
   That absolutely *nobody commits*.
   It is *discipleship that costs nothing*.
   And it is all done in hopes that:

- Society will be *impressed* at how devout we are.
- God will be *impressed* at how self-loathing we are.
- The Church will *grow* hand over fist.

But this inauthentic repentance impresses no one.
   Because deep down?
   None of us actually believe anyone alive is guilty of anything
historical.
   Because *nobody alive today* was involved in the Crusades, or the
Salem Witch Trials, or colonial conquest.
   But the apology tour continues.
   Because it's not about justice.
   It's about control.
   And that?
   That is the very essence of Babel.

God's Reversal

And so, in the great irony of history, God does *not* use the self-flag-ellating, self-loathing Babel builders to continue His mission on earth.

Instead?

He finds a man in the desert.

A man whose best years are behind him.

A man who doesn't even *want* to start over.

A man who has nothing to offer—except faith.

God rejects the youth of the world—

And He chooses Abram.

Because Abram will listen.

Abram will believe.

Abram will not build towers.

Abram will not try to manipulate God.

And that?

That is what God is looking for.

And that is *still* what God is looking for.

"Blame the Church" Is a Lazy Game

"Our states are failed because Christianity oppressed us."

Except—

These states were failed long before the Christians ever arrived.

And when Christians were there?

They prospered.

And when Christians left?

They collapsed—back into their former corruption.

Blame the Church is a fun game—

But it is dishonest.

And history has a long memory.

Blaming the Church is the theological equivalent of blaming your personal trainer for your weight gain—while eating a cheeseburger and washing it down with a two-liter of Mountain Dew. The Church brought literacy, charity, education, and systems of justice where there was none, yet revisionist history has a convenient way of writing those contributions out.

You know who didn't invent hospitals? Pagans. You know who didn't codify human rights into law? The Secularists. You know who didn't advocate for the dignity of every person, regardless of status or wealth? The pre-Christian world. But now? Now the same civilization that birthed every major social good in the modern era is suddenly the villain because of... I don't know, a bad PR team? A Twitter scandal?

And these?

These thrown-together structures—hastily assembled, built on half-baked ideology and sentimental virtue-signaling—

They will eventually be abandoned.

Because they are deeply disingenuous.

Because they are ultimately a heap of social trash.

Because they offer nothing that can't be found in a university lecture or a trending TikTok sermon.

The Babel Church isn't countercultural.

It's redundant.

And nobody—not the world, not the faithful—wants a redundant church.

The Pattern: God's Blueprint for Building

God told Moses to construct the Tabernacle according to the pattern shown to him on the Mount of God.

This was the guiding principle of Israel's political history:

Do things God's way.

Not Rome's way.

Not Babylon's way.

Not the way of the latest Ted Talk or business leadership seminar.

And that same principle extends into the New Testament Church.

But what do we do?

We keep grabbing the bricks of Babel and trying to retrofit them into the Kingdom of God like some kind of divine IKEA hack. We tell ourselves we're "contextualizing," when in reality, we're just compromise-washing. "If we could just tweak the message a little, make it a little softer, a little more palatable, people will listen!" Meanwhile, Jesus said, "Eat my flesh and drink my blood," and people left in droves.

Turns out, God doesn't care about marketing strategies.

He cares about faithfulness.

Abraham: The Man Who Listened

This is why God leapt at Abram—

Because he believed God's words.

Not because he was looking to make a name for himself.

Not because he had the right credentials.

Not because he had built a massive platform on Instagram.

Because he listened.

God didn't choose Abraham because he had the most potential. He wasn't a 22-year-old Harvard dropout coding in his dorm room, about to disrupt the financial industry. He was 75. He didn't have time to disrupt anything except maybe a dinner party by falling asleep too early.

But that's exactly who God picks.

He picks the old guy that the world is done with. The one that isn't a safe bet. The one who knows that if anything great is going to happen, it will be God—not him—who does it.

And that's the problem with the Babel Church.

It believes it can do this without God.

Faith of the Ear

Christians are meant to be people of the ear.

Not the eye.

Not the vibe.

Not the TEDx-adjacent leadership principles.

We possess Abrahamic faith.

And Abrahamic faith is:

An ear that hears God and a heart that believes Him, no matter how incredulous or culturally foreign the Word sounds.

Abraham didn't crowdsource his faith.

God kept violating Abraham's cultural sensibilities—

And Abraham kept believing.

"Leave your country."

"The promise will come through Sarah."

"Sacrifice your heir."

And somehow, Abraham kept saying yes.

Why?

Because he believed in something higher than the latest social theory or the pressures of popular consensus. He wasn't building Babel. He was waiting for something better.

Abraham's Dead Old Faith

Abraham was a faithful witness to God's power and sovereignty—

Even in his imperfect obedience.

And this?

This is the place the Church needs to return to.

Dead old faith.

The kind of faith that doesn't worry about aesthetics.

The kind of faith that isn't branding itself for the algorithm.

The kind of faith that doesn't chase cultural relevance like a desperate ex.

It's when you're out of options.

It's when you stop caring about reinventing yourself.

It's when you abandon attempts at fruitfulness outside of God's sovereign plan that brings Him glory.

Abrahamic faith says:

"I'm not laying bricks with the masses. I have rejected their bricks. I want nothing to do with what they are building."

A City Built by God

Hebrews tells us that Abraham looked for a city whose founder and builder was God.

Which is fascinating, considering where Abraham was from.

Because Abraham grew up in Ur—

Home to one of the largest ziggurats ever discovered by archaeologists.

He lived through one of the most exciting periods in ancient architectural history.

He saw human innovation at its peak.

"Wow, look at this insane mound of dirt we made! The gods will have to work for us now! Life is gonna be amazing."

But where does Abraham end up?

Living in tents.

Abraham: The City Boy in the Desert

Imagine the irony:
  Abraham is a city boy—
  Dragged out to the middle of nowhere—
  Because his stupid dad decided to leave Ur and settle in a mid-tier river town.
  And then?
  He spends the rest of his life in tents.
  Even after he starts following God.
  Abraham probably would have preferred a penthouse in downtown Ur. But God had other plans. Plans that required trust over convenience, faith over familiarity.

The Quiet Part Out Loud

The book of Hebrews is saying the quiet part out loud:
  Abraham didn't want to be in tents.
  When things got tough?
  He ran to cities.
  But cities never worked out for him.
  Human innovation always let him down.
  It was through YHWH's blessing that his life actually started to take off.
  Not through the power of the city.
  Not through the power of innovation.
  Not through the power of Babel.

Babel Bricks & Church-Building

God needs to give us the eyes of Abraham—
  Eyes that mock Babel bricks.

Eyes that see what Moses saw when he wrote Genesis—
And laughed.

"What the heck am I building, God?"

"What bricks am I using?"

"What cultural breakthroughs or societal gold standards am I relying on to build something for You—when they are actually just a pile of rubbish?"

Because the Church isn't mine.

It isn't yours.

It isn't anybody's.

The Church belongs to Jesus.

So if we're going to build something that lasts?

We better build it His way.

Chapter Four

The Joseph Church

When I moved to New York City in 2010, I lived with two Australians—Joel Houston and Dylan Thomas.

It was Joel's apartment—corner of Lafayette and Grand in SoHo—and Dylan and I were sleeping on the floor like the homeless squatters that we were.

We thought we'd won the lottery—

Not because of comfort—but because Joel let us stay for free.

The location? Unreal.

The SoHo Sessions

Every afternoon, Dylan and I would sit around the long wooden table in the apartment, drinking coffee, thumbing a poorly intonated Baby Taylor, and staring down at the bustling Manhattan streets.

One day, in the middle of one of these sessions, we started talking about recording some songs together.

That week?

We wrote three more songs and decided to head to Canada to record them with my friend David.

We took the train to Toronto, recorded music for a week, came back to NYC, and then—next month—flew to Europe to play in Brooke Fraser's band for twelve dates.

It was the kind of thing that, if you squinted at it from the right angle, felt like divine orchestration.

A seamless unfolding of opportunities.

Like the universe had been waiting for us to say "yes."

Or maybe we were just young, untethered, and unreasonably confident.

(Confidence is the currency of the clueless.)

Stories That Anchor Us

When I think of Dylan, my mind defaults to those early days.

Our life was making music together.

Today, Dylan lives in Franklin, TN—right around the corner from me.

And we are still making music together.

For years, we didn't. But in my mind?

Dylan is forever that brilliant guitar player, songwriter, and tastemaker.

And no matter where we are in life, or how much time has passed—

I have these wild stories of Dylan:

- The late nights in Manhattan.
- The day off in Amsterdam where we almost got killed by bicycles.
- Getting pizza in Bondi late at night.
- Snowboarding at Whistler B.C.

These are core memories.

They hold everything between us in place.

They remind me that even when people drift—when life separates us—history holds us together.

Because stories do more than entertain.

They define the space between us.

Stories vs. Facts

I used to think stories were just entertainment—things we tell to amuse ourselves.

I had divided the world into two categories:

- **Facts**—used to arm ourselves.
- **Stories**—used to entertain ourselves.

But the reverse is true.
People arm themselves with stories—
And they entertain themselves with facts.
Because stories shape identity.
They form culture.
They give us purpose, meaning, and context for navigating the symbols and signs we encounter every single day.
This is why propaganda works.
This is why people are willing to die for causes that, on a purely logical level, make zero sense.
The facts of a situation don't matter.
The story being told does.

A Canadian in Rome

Today, I'm a Canadian in Rome.
This morning, I ordered an omelette at Café Rosati in Piazza del Popolo.
And, in a bold act of culinary defiance, I asked for an insalata mista to go with my already preposterous request for eggs.
The waiter looked up from his notepad, stared at me over his spectacles, and said:
"You know you're in Rome, right?"

I nodded.

He sighed. Wrote it down anyway.

But his whole body language was saying: *This man is lost. He is a danger to himself and others.*

Clashing Cultural Narratives

Of course I know I'm in Rome.

But I'm Canadian, and we don't eat chocolate cornetti for breakfast.

Pastries?

That's what fat losers like me eat for breakfast.

I need protein—so I can be a skinny boy again.

Except—

The problem with that story is that I am, in fact, a fat loser right now.

Meanwhile, Romans get away with eating pastries for breakfast because they get 40,000 steps a day.

I tell myself the story that eliminating carbs and sugar will make me skinny.

Romans tell themselves the story that if they give up carbs and sugar, they might as well give up on life.

The facts don't matter to either of us.

What matters is the story we believe.

And here's the kicker:

Neither of our stories is entirely true.

That's the thing about narratives.

They help us interpret the world—

But they can also be deceptive.

Just ask Joseph.

The Power of National Stories

People don't just have personal stories—countries and organizations do too. And many times, those stories are even more potent, capable of shaping national identities, public policies, and even the subconscious moral compass of an entire civilization. The great political fights of our time? They aren't just about policy. They're about competing narratives. Who gets to tell the story? Who decides the lens through which we view history? Who determines what events mean?

Take the American Revolutionary War, for example. It's not just history—it's a culturally formative story. It's the legend that breathes life into the American psyche, shaping everything from how citizens interpret government power to why they keep buying firearms like they're the last surviving cast member of *Red Dawn*. The American Constitution is read through the lens of this founding narrative. America rebelled against tyranny, so every law must preserve the people's right to rebel against oppression. This is why the Second Amendment isn't just about gun ownership; it's about identity. It's about the right to stand up and say, *We will never be ruled again.*

Now, contrast that with a place like Canada—where national identity is more about *not* being American, drinking Tim Hortons, and apologizing when someone steps on *your* foot. The stories nations tell themselves matter. They set the trajectory for everything—how people vote, what they believe, what they think is possible.

The 1619 Project & National Mythology

This is why the **1619 Project** doesn't need to be historically accurate to be culturally formative. Like Homer's *Iliad*, it is a *mythos*—a grand, sweeping narrative designed not merely to inform, but to inspire a particular moral vision. It's not an academic paper; it's a cultural sledgehammer.

Conservatives can tear it apart all they want. They can roll out credentialed historians who disassemble the thesis brick by brick, footnote by footnote. But none of that matters, because facts alone don't build cultures—stories do. If a narrative taps into an already-existing sense of grievance or identity, it will spread like wildfire, regardless of how many scholarly journals issue polite rebuttals.

We see this dynamic play out in places like Northern Ireland, where Protestants and Catholics aren't just fighting about theology (spoiler: they aren't really fighting about theology at all). They are fighting over competing national stories. One group tells the story of British identity, monarchy, and Protestant work ethic. The other tells a story of colonial oppression, resilience, and Irish sovereignty. And at this point, the actual historical *facts* of past events barely matter—it's the story each side believes about themselves that fuels the division.

This is the power of narrative. If moving forward together is the goal, what's required isn't another history lesson. What's required is a new story—a story that both sides can share.

The Exodus Story: Israel's National Identity

No nation has understood the power of story quite like **Israel**. The most powerful story in their history is the **Exodus**—not merely a tale of divine rescue, but the very bedrock of Jewish identity. Every Passover, every prayer, every festival is a retelling, a reminder, a reinforcement of this foundational narrative: *We were slaves in Egypt, and YHWH delivered us with a mighty hand and an outstretched arm.*

It shaped their spiritual life—God is a liberator.

It shaped their political life—No foreign king shall rule over us.

It shaped their social life—We must care for the stranger, because we too were strangers in Egypt.

This is why Israel, as a people, has endured for thousands of years, while countless other ancient civilizations have crumbled into dust. No other people have maintained their cultural distinctives with such accuracy and zeal. And why? Because they have a story—a story stronger than exile, stronger than persecution, stronger than every empire that has tried to erase them.

But here's the fascinating thing:

For the actual individuals who escaped Egypt, their foundational story wasn't *Exodus*. It was **Joseph**.

Genesis: The Story That Held Israel Together

Moses had a job. A hard one.

He had to take a ragtag group of recently liberated Hebrew slaves and unify them into a cohesive nation. How? Through **story**.

He had to record YHWH's self-revelation as the one true God, dismantling the polytheistic assumptions of Egyptian mythology. He had to give the people a past—not just a past of suffering, but a past of **promise**. He had to remind them that they weren't an accident of history, but the fulfillment of **YHWH's covenant with Abraham**.

This is why Genesis—**not Exodus**—was the true **origin document** of Israel's faith. Genesis wasn't just an ancient history lesson. It was a **binding legal document**, a spiritual deed of ownership that declared:

> *You are not Egyptians. You are not Babylonian. You are not just runaway slaves. You are Abraham's children, Isaac's descendants, Jacob's heirs.*

And most importantly:

You are the people of YHWH.

And when Moses got to Joseph's story, **he slowed down**.

Why? Because the story of **Joseph** was critical for Israel's self-understanding.

Why Joseph?

Joseph gets **fourteen chapters** in Genesis—the same amount of real estate as **Abraham**. That's not an accident.

Because the Joseph story gave Israel:

- **A backbone**—they were a people long before Pharaoh enslaved them.
- **A purpose**—their suffering wasn't because they were weak or inferior, but because they were divinely set apart.
- **A sense of supernatural destiny**—Joseph didn't rise because of his own brilliance, but because YHWH was with him.

And this story wasn't just a relic of the past. Throughout Israel's history—whether in exile, rebuilding, or waiting—the Joseph story was **repeated**. Because it reminded them of a deeper truth:

The nation that welcomes us is saved. The nation that rejects us is destroyed.

Because Israel wasn't just a people.
They belonged to a **warrior God**.
And the secret to their corporate power?

Was the same secret to Joseph's power:
Remaining a **faithful witness** to YHWH—**even in exile**.

The Joseph Church: Living as Exiles

Fast forward to the early Church—
Under the thumb of the Roman Empire.
Persecuted. Hunted. Mistrusted.
Viewed as subversive, dangerous, and weird.
The early Church was a veritable **Joseph**—

- Cast into the pit.
- Made up of the slaves and nobodies of the Empire.
- Under the constant threat of death.

They had no social capital, no army, no government backing.
With nothing but their faith in Christ to give them irrational hope in overwhelming darkness.
And yet—
Like Joseph,
Like Israel,
Like every exile before them—
They **flourished**.

Faithful Witness: The Prophetic Call

John's prophetic vision in *Revelation* wasn't meant to be some cosmic horror movie script.

It wasn't a doom-scroll for paranoid prepper Christians.

It was **encouragement**—to persecuted believers, spread throughout the Empire.

A major theme of *Revelation*?

Faithful Witness.

Remain committed to Christ—come hell or high water.

Jesus Himself is introduced as **The Faithful Witness** (*Rev. 1:13*).

And the question is posed:

Will we **worship the Beast** in exchange for socio-economic mobility?

Or will we **love not our lives even unto death** and remain **faithful witnesses**?

This is the question of our time.

Because **every age** demands a choice.

Every **Christian generation** will be confronted with its own Babylon.

Every follower of Jesus will have their own *Joseph moment*—

A moment to bow to the system—

Or remain a **faithful witness**.

And if history tells us anything?

It's that the faithful witnesses—the ones who refuse to worship the idols of their age—

Are the ones God uses to change the world.

The Joseph Church in the Last Days

I see incredible prophetic application in the story of Joseph—its culturally formative power for ancient Israel and its fulfillment in the Church—

The Israel of God (Gal. 6:16).

The Joseph Church, then, is a Church under the thumb of the Empire—

Sent as a sentinel into the heart of the Beast to save it or destroy it.

I believe the Last Days Church is a **Joseph Church**—

Not a cloistered, retreating, self-preserving institution, but a **Church embedded in the chaos** of a failing world—

Literally **saving the people of the Empire** while being resented for doing so.

The Joseph Church is an eschatological Church—

Not obsessed with doom, but armed with divine strategy.

Prophecy as Core Function, Not Fringe Feature

Gordon Fee argues that the charisms are the defining marks of the Church in the eschaton—

And if a Church doesn't practice them,

It isn't operating in its present calling.

"Your sons and daughters will prophesy."

Not a bug.

Not an optional feature.

This is baked into the DNA of the Joseph Church because it is crucial to its mission.

But here's where the Western Church has blundered:

It has relegated prophecy to a **charismatic niche**, a weird corner of the Church full of shofars, end-times charts, and YouTube conspiracy videos about microchips.

Meanwhile, biblical prophecy isn't about speculating on barcodes and vaccines—

It's about **receiving divine insight for the moment at hand**.

Joseph interpreted Pharaoh's dream—not to **frighten Egypt into prepping for the apocalypse,**

But to **save it from collapse**.

And the Last Days Joseph Church must do the same.

It must rise above **fear-driven theology** and embrace **prophetic wisdom**—

Guiding **nations, economies, and cultures** through divine insight rather than **panicked reactionism**.

The Political Friction of a Favored Son

The Church is the favored son—
A people marked by divine fruitfulness and historical impact.
And just like Joseph—
It has **caused political friction**.
Joseph's favor **drove his brothers to rage**.
He was **hated for his dreams** before he was hated for his position.
His mere existence **threatened their control over the narrative**.
The **Joseph Church** is similarly accused today:

- "You think you have the truth?"
- "You think you hear from God?"
- "You think you have a moral authority to speak into culture?"

Yes. Yes. And yes.
This is not **arrogance**—this is **inheritance**.
The Church's fruitfulness **isn't self-produced**; it is **divinely appointed**.
And just as Joseph's brothers **couldn't erase his favor**,
The secular world **cannot erase the Church's impact**—
Though it will try.

Blaming the Church: A Revisionist Sport

Secularism and Liberalism are failing.
Someone must be blamed.
And the Church is the easiest target—
Because of the **revisionist stories** we tell ourselves about it.

"The Church is oppressive!" →   It has, in fact, been the **great liberator** of souls and societies.

"The Church is exclusive!" →   It is the **most multiethnic** movement in history.

"The Church is racist!" →   It is predominantly **Global South**, founded on documents written by **Jews**.

And yet here we are—

Blaming the Church for the obvious **moral collapse** wrought by the Enlightenment's false promises.

This is the irony of modern secular culture:

It *wants* the moral world Christianity created—

But *hates* the moral lawgiver that established it.

The Church: Political Pawn, Eternal Enemy

The Church has always been **used politically**—

Just like Joseph was used by Potiphar.

It keeps the peace.

It encourages stability.

It tells the **Right** to work hard and pay taxes.

It tells the **Left** to remember the poor and vulnerable.

The **Church does the political work of the Right-Left binary**—

Yet is **always under the foot of the State**.

When the State succeeds, the **State is praised**.

When the State fails, the **Church is blamed**.

It is an **eternal enemy** because it **will not disappear**.

Every empire that has tried to erase it—

Has collapsed.

Because **Joseph always rises**.

Morality: Still a Christian Invention

Every modern political debate is a **moral debate**—
　And every moral debate is **implicitly Christian**.
　"Which political party is more moral?"
　This is how Westerners vote.
　But whose morality are they appealing to?
　Judeo-Christian morality.
　Every single time.
　The Church **completely reshaped** the world's moral landscape.
　There is **no going back**.
　Yes—there are perversions of Christianity.
　But they are still **Christian perversions**.

Potiphar's Wife & The Sexual Revolution

A great drama has played out in the Church's socio-political role:
　Potiphar's wife—
　Typified by the **Sexual Revolution**—
　Has **tempted the Joseph Church**.
　And the **Joseph Church** has **categorically rejected her**.
　And **hell hath no fury like a woman scorned**.
　The modern West cannot **stand the Church** for one reason:
　It **will not bow** to its ever-shifting sexual doctrines.
　It will **not approve** of unrestricted sexuality.
　It will **not affirm** that sin is a human right.
　It will **not participate** in cultural amnesia,
　Pretending that **biblical morality** was a historical accident
　And that human progress has finally "transcended" it.
　Joseph **fled from Potiphar's wife**—
　And ended up **in a dungeon** because of it.

Likewise, the Church is **canceled, vilified, censored, and silenced**

Because it will not give up its moral inheritance.

The Postmodernist Rebellion: A War Against God's Law

At the root of **Postmodernism's rejection** of meta-narratives
Wasn't a **noble search for truth**—
It was a **desire to have sex without consequence.**
Marx provided the **paradigm** they needed:
The winners wrote the rules, and Christianity had won.
If the **Church made the rules**,
Then **morality was just a form of control**.
Thus:

- There is **no God**.
- There is **no lawgiver**.
- **Conscience is a social construct**.
- **Morality is oppression**.

Sexual liberation became an act of political defiance.
The **Sexual Revolution**—
A brainchild of **Enlightenment thought** and **Postmodernist philosophy**—
Exploded like a rocket.
But the **Joseph Church?**
The **Joseph Church did not budge**.
The **Joseph Church refused the invitation**
To **adulterate itself** with the cultural moment.
And **for this**,
It is **hated by the world**.
But the world forgets—

That **Joseph's story doesn't end in the dungeon**.
It ends in a palace.
And **so will the Church's**.

Porn & the New Pagans: The Church in Exile

Yes—our culture has sexualized us in ways unimaginable. We aren't living on an Amish farm anymore, where the most scandalous image was an exposed ankle on laundry day. We are inundated— everywhere—from advertisements to entertainment to fashion to algorithms that know exactly how to hijack the male brain. Even pagans of old would blush at the scale.

Jordan Peterson remarked somewhere online that the average Western male who watches pornography regularly has seen more naked women in five minutes than his great grandfather did in his entire lifetime.[3] That should stop us in our tracks. Solomon—the man with 700 wives and 300 concubines—saw less nudity than a dude with WiFi and a moment of boredom. We have crossed some kind of threshold that even the kings of antiquity never could have imagined.

But here's the kicker—pagans of old *wanted* a society obsessed with sex. They carved it into temple walls, created fertility cults, and built entire mythologies around it. The new pagans? They pretend to be shocked by it. They promote it while simultaneously condemning the consequences. "Sexual liberation for all! But also, purity culture was *really damaging!*" The cognitive dissonance is

---

[3] In a 2018 article titled "Jordan Peterson and Powerful Men," Alastair Roberts notes that "a man today can see more naked women in five minutes than his great grandfather could see in a lifetime," a quotation from Peterson in some interview he gave that this author could not track down, as the many pericope of Peterson litter social media like water bottles in a Haitian river. This is a particularly salient point: access to naked women is destroying the male psyche—we don't have the hardware needed to process this kind of stimulation.

staggering. They cheer on the normalization of kinks that would have made Caligula blush—then act bewildered when relationships fall apart and mental illness spikes.

The Church in Political Prison

The Joseph Church has remained faithful. We have rejected Potiphar's wife. And now? She is furious.

Her revenge? Cast the Church into the lower parts of society. We are now prisoners in a cultural exile.

Not because we failed.

Not because we were hypocrites.

Not because we lost an election.

Not because we lacked innovation.

But because we refused to bow.

And now? We are in a **social prison**.

We have lost access to cultural power.

We are peripheral.

We are not invited to the table.

We are considered dangerous for merely *existing*.

But here's the critical part—**this is God's doing.**

The prison wasn't our failure. The prison was our faithfulness. We said "no" to the empire's demands. And the empire does not forgive. But neither does God forget.

The Prophetic Blindness of This Generation

What is driving me mad is the absolute lack of prophetic wherewithal in young leaders. They don't know anything in Scripture outside of Matthew 5–7, and even that they interpret through the lens of self-help psychology. They quote Micah 6:8, but couldn't tell you a thing about Micah's actual life. They want *Jeremiah*

29:11, but have never read the rest of Jeremiah—the suffering prophet, the man whose life was a catastrophe of obedience.

You cannot prophesy if you do not know Scripture.

The office of the prophet was never about untethered mystical predictions—

It was a **call back** to Mosaic memory.

A *repetition* of divine law.

"This is what God has said."

Not just "This is what God is saying."

Prophecy is more of a call *back* than a call *forward*. And if we fail to see that—if we sever prophecy from biblical memory—then we will **fail to see what God is doing now**. We will misread the moment. We will interpret cultural exile as failure instead of faithfulness.

The Hard Word: The Prophetic Cost

God put Joseph in the prison because He knew Joseph would give the hard word to the Baker.

The Hard Word is the Biblical Prophetic Exhortation that nobody wants to give.

Because it is disruptive.

Because it is costly.

Because it makes you the enemy of the moment—no matter how lovingly it's delivered.

It's the *Mission: Impossible* of prophetic assignments.

It's what cost John the Baptist his head.

It's what got Jesus crucified.

It's what got all the disciples murdered.

It's what filled the stakes of *Foxe's Book of Martyrs*.

It's the romanticized one-way ticket to a comet hurtling toward Earth, where you have to plant the nuke to save the world while Steven Tyler screeches *I Don't Wanna Miss a Thing* in the background.

Nobody wants that job.

But God is merciful—

And He desires to **warn a dying people**.

To **demonstrate His love**.

To **execute His hidden plans of salvation**.

And so, He sends prophets.

Not to *win*—but to *warn*.

Not to *gain power*—but to *give clarity*.

The Faithful Witness & the Fearless Word

Faithful Witnesses do not modify the word to make it palatable.

They deliver it in love—

But they cannot control its impact.

They don't care where it lands them—financially, socially, politically.

They don't care about fallout.

They care only about obeying God.

Joseph resisted Potiphar's wife—

And it *won* him his ministry in the prison.

It wasn't a **demotion**. It was a **promotion**.

Because it was in the prison where Pharaoh would find him.

Excellence in the Pit: The Joseph Church's Posture

Joseph is in the prison.

Perfectly positioned by God—though he doesn't know it yet.

And what does he do?

Does he sit in despair?

Does he sulk in his suffering?

Does he write a 30-tweet thread about deconstruction?
No.
He **functions with an excellent spirit**.
He administrates the prison.
He serves his fellow inmates.
Joseph's ministry hasn't changed.
Only his **recipients** have.
He was faithful in Potiphar's house.
Now he is faithful in Pharaoh's prison.
And **this is the posture of the Joseph Church**.
We do not **whine**.
We **work**.
We do not **retreat**.
We **serve**.
We do not **pander**.
We **prophesy**.

The Joseph Church & the Underclass

The Joseph Church does not pander to the **Rich Young Ruler**—
Who can't afford association with us because of **bad publicity optics**.
Instead, we faithfully minister to the **lowly**.
To the **forgotten**.
To the **prisoners of society**.
Because in faithfulness to the assignment,
God will bring the promotion.
To the highest places of the land.
For the salvation of the elect.

The Hard Word & the Forgotten Prophet

The Baker and Cupbearer have dreams.

They know Joseph's prophetic gift—because he **practices** it.

So they ask him for interpretation.

And the Lord gives the meaning.

For one of them?

The interpretation is brutal.

And Joseph delivers it **anyway**.

No sugar-coating.

No hedging.

No "Well, it's unclear, let's pray some more."

He gives the **hard word**.

And then?

Joseph is forgotten.

Because **Pharaoh must first dream**—and be in desperation.

Because **Pharaoh must first exhaust his own counselors and magicians**.

Pharaoh must see the limits of his own human wisdom.

And **only then** will the Joseph Church be remembered.

This is our posture.

This is our assignment.

We are not fighting for *cultural recognition*.

We are *waiting for Pharaoh to dream*.

And when he does?

We will be ready.

The Joseph Church & the Political Moment

Joseph is taken to the palace—quickly.

One moment he's in the dungeon, the next he's being shaved, washed, dressed in royal robes. The transformation is almost laughable in its speed. Yesterday, he was in rags. Today, he stands before the most powerful man on earth. It's a Hollywood moment before Hollywood existed.

And this is where most of us would mess up.

We would see the opportunity. We would see the power at play. And we would think, *This is my shot. Don't blow it. Make it palatable.*

The temptation? To play the game. To soften the edges. To give Pharaoh what he wants, or at least something digestible.

But Joseph does not.

He gives the hard word.

"Seven years of plenty."

"Seven years of famine."

No sugarcoating. No hedging. No trying to be Pharaoh's buddy. Just the facts, given with the confidence that they are from God Himself.

Joseph knows what so many of us forget:

The truth doesn't need permission to be true.

Good News Has Bad News First

The Joseph Church has good news.

But it also carries bad news.

And here's the thing—we want to skip past the bad news. We want to rush to the salvation part. We want to say, *Jesus loves you* without saying, *You're a sinner in need of salvation.*

We want *grace* without *repentance.*

We want *redemption* without *reckoning.*

But the gospel is only "good news" because the bad news is actually bad.

And only the Joseph Church—only a people who can stand before power and say what *God* says—can administrate salvation on the earth. Only the Joseph Church can be trusted with political influence, because it understands that power exists not for self-preservation, but for *preserving life.*

The Problem with Pessimistic Eschatology

Somewhere along the way, we bought into this idea that the Church is supposed to die like a failing business.

That it's supposed to dwindle, collapse, and disappear—because, you know, "the world is getting worse."

What kind of defeatist theology is this? What kind of spineless eschatology makes us think that a thriving, society-shaping Church is a *compromised* Church?

Since when was victory a problem?

Yes, we know persecution will come. Yes, we know there will be hardship. But last time I checked, Jesus didn't say, *The gates of the Church will not prevail against the world.*

He said:

> *"I will build My Church, and the gates of hell shall not prevail against it."*

Hell is the one on defense. The Church is supposed to be raiding it.

But instead, many Christians have adopted a theology of retreat. A belief that we should get smaller, weaker, and less involved, all while muttering something about how "it's all going to burn anyway."

Except—

God has always preserved His people *in judgment.*

God's Preservation of the Joseph Church

Take the Jerusalem Church in A.D. 70.

Rome laid siege to the city for four years. Jerusalem was a pressure cooker of starvation, infighting, and devastation. Finally, the Romans broke through. The Temple was destroyed. 1.1 million Jews were slaughtered.

But the Church?

Did it die with the city?

No.

Because God warned them.

F.F. Bruce notes that according to Eusebius, the Church received a prophetic word *before the war*—a divine instruction to flee to Pella.[4]

And they did.

They left before the siege. They survived.

Not because they were lucky. Not because they were smarter than everyone else.

But because God preserved them.

Because God does not delight in His people perishing.

Because *the Joseph Church listens when God speaks.*

Jonah, the Hard Word & the Possibility of Repentance

But maybe there's another angle here.

---

[4] In his work *The Early Church*, F.F. Bruce references the account by the fourth-century historian Eusebius, who recorded that the Jerusalem church received an oracle instructing them to flee to Pella prior to the city's destruction in 70 AD. This event is detailed in Eusebius's *Ecclesiastical History*, Book 3, Chapter 5. But seriously think about that—if you're worried about the End of the World, let this story encourage you: God is going to communicate with His people prophetically in the coming days in order to lead and guide and save.

Maybe the real takeaway isn't just survival—it's *repentance.*

Because when God sends a hard word, it's not just to say, *Brace for impact.* It's also to say, *Turn and live.*

Take Nineveh.

Jonah showed up and preached the most apathetic sermon in history.

"Yet forty days, and Nineveh shall be overthrown."

That's it. No altar call. No hopeful conclusion. No emotional music playing in the background.

And yet—*the city repented.*

Because the word of the Lord came.

And the people *believed* it.

They didn't argue. They didn't say, *Well, that's just your interpretation, Jonah.* They heard the warning, they recognized it as true, and they repented.

And here's what's crazy:

Jonah *didn't even want them to repent.*

He was hoping they would ignore him so God would nuke the place.

But they repented anyway.

Why We Shy Away from the Hard Word

And this is why we shy away from the hard word.

We don't actually believe people will listen.

We don't believe in repentance.

We don't believe in the power of God to *change hearts.*

So we modify the message. We make it softer, safer. We try to package it in a way that won't offend, as if the gospel is *less* powerful if it's *more* truthful.

And when that happens?

We become the Babel Church.

We start *building our own version of Christianity*—one that people will accept, one that Pharaoh will nod along with, one that the world won't be too upset about.

And in doing so, we *rob* people of the opportunity to truly repent.

The Joseph Church Speaks Because It Believes

The Joseph Church is a *prophetic* Church.

It knows Scripture.

It knows the voice of God.

It believes in the power of God.

And because it believes—

It *speaks.*

It does not shy away. It does not modify. It does not wait until it's *politically convenient* to tell the truth.

Because it knows that *the power of God is not in the packaging.*

It's in the *proclamation.*

Oh God, Raise Up a Joseph Church

A Church that knows it is being positioned for a *great salvation.*

A Church that will *not shrink back.*

A Church that sees the *prophetic moment.*

A Church that *delivers the hard word.*

A Church that *trusts in the power of God.*

Oh God, raise up a **Joseph Church** in these last days.

Chapter Five
The Joshua Church

In **Numbers 13:16 – 14:9**, we find ourselves at a pivotal moment in Israel's journey. So far, they've been delivered from Egypt, led across the Red Sea, and given the first-ever crash course in *YHWH is Not Like Other Gods 101*. They've witnessed some of the greatest supernatural flexes in history—water shooting out of a rock like a fire hydrant, chicken wings raining from the sky, waffle batter misting the ground every morning.

No generation has had this level of acute God-awareness. They've seen things even the disciples didn't see—the Nile transforming into a river of blood, frogs going full apocalypse-mode, hail obliterating Egyptian crops, and an honest-to-goodness pillar of fire leading them like a divine GPS. God's presence hasn't been subtle. It's been neon, Vegas-level obvious.

And yet, despite all of this, despite miracles that would make even the most committed cynic sit up and reconsider their life choices, their journey through the wilderness—a trip that should have been short and sweet—is about to morph into a generational detour.

Canaan: God's Land, God's Eviction Notice

Canaan isn't just some random real estate—this is God's land. He owns it. He holds the deed. And He's evicting the current tenants. Why? Because the people living there have reached peak moral bankruptcy.

Look at **Genesis 15:13-16**, where God tells Abram:

> *"Know for certain that your offspring will be sojourners in a land that is not theirs and will be servants there, and they will be afflicted for four hundred years. But I will bring judgment on the nation that they serve, and afterward they shall come out with great possessions... And they shall come back here in the fourth generation, for the iniquity of the Amorites is not yet complete."*

Translation: God isn't just randomly obliterating nations—He's extraordinarily patient. He waited four *centuries* for the Amorites and their Canaanite cousins to change course. They didn't. In fact, their depravity went from bad to worse. So now, Israel is moving in.

And lest they get too comfortable—if Israel starts acting like the people they're replacing, they too will be evicted. Spoiler alert: this exact thing happens **hundreds of years later** when Babylon marches in and levels Jerusalem like it's a Jenga tower in a hurricane.

The Nephilim Problem

So Moses sends twelve spies into Canaan—one from each tribe. Before they leave, Moses does something interesting: he changes Hoshea's name to **Joshua** (from "He Saves" to "YHWH Saves"). That's a theological flex before the battle even begins.

When the spies return, their report starts off solid:

> *"Yeah, the land is ridiculous. It's flowing with milk and honey. The grapes are so massive that two of us had to carry a single cluster on a pole."*

This is the exact visual God wanted. It's meant to get the people hyped. They should be foaming at the mouth with excitement, like toddlers in the back of a minivan when someone hands them a juice box.

Instead? **Full-scale meltdown.**

Because right after describing the land's insane fertility, the spies shift gears:

> *"Okay, yeah, milk and honey, but the people are huge. Their cities are fortified and massive. And, uh, also—we saw the descendants of Anak there."*

At this point, **Caleb** steps up and tries to rally the troops:

> *"Let's go up now and take it, for we are well able to overcome it."*

You love to see it. Caleb's got that old-school, David-before-Goliath, unflinching faith. He's ready to roll. But the other ten spies? Immediate panic attack.

> *"We will get wrecked. The land devours its inhabitants. Everyone there is gigantic. And the worst part? We saw the Nephilim—the sons of Anak, who come from the Nephilim. And compared to them? We looked like grasshoppers."*

That last line is key. This isn't just normal fear—this is an existential, "we're-about-to-get-wiped-off-the-map" level of terror.

Who Are the Nephilim?

If you've ever read Frank Peretti or binge-watched *Ancient Aliens*, you already know what's up. These are giants.

Goliath? A descendant of Anak.

Dude was **nine feet tall** and **a trained killer**.

But this goes deeper. We have to rewind back to **Genesis 6**, a chapter so bonkers it reads like the opening scene of a supernatural horror film.

Genesis 6 describes a period when *elohim* (spiritual beings) came down from heaven and started *hooking up* with human women, producing **a hybrid race of monstrous warriors**.

The **Nephilim**.

They weren't just tall—they were freakishly powerful, supernaturally twisted, and absolute murder machines. They terrorized the earth. The situation got so out of control that **God hit the reset button**—hence, the flood.

So now, here's the unsettling question:

If the flood wiped out all the Nephilim…

…**how are they still around in Moses' day?**

Wait—Didn't They Drown?

That's the terrifying mystery. **Numbers explicitly links the Anakim to the Nephilim.**

Which means—

Somehow, some way, the Nephilim *survived*.

How? Theories abound.

Some scholars believe their DNA made it through via **Noah's family line**—not because Noah himself was corrupted, but possibly through one of his sons' wives. Others think **the fallen sons of God pulled a repeat stunt post-flood**, which would explain why these giants are still kicking around Canaan like some kind of **post-apocalyptic demigods**.[5]

---

[5] In Frank Peretti's novel *Monster* (2005), there is a creature that some characters initially believe to be a Bigfoot/Sasquatch-type entity, but the story later reveals deeper implications about

Either way—
These guys are back.
And Israel?
They're supposed to fight them.

Faith vs. Fear

This is the moment of decision. Israel stands on the edge of the Promised Land, faced with a choice:

1. **Trust God**—believe that the same God who split the Red Sea and turned Pharaoh into a glorified meme can handle a few oversized warriors.
2. **Collapse in fear**—convince themselves they're doomed, run for the hills, and guarantee a whole lot of desert-wandering.

And unfortunately, we already know how this story ends.

Caleb and Joshua are ready to charge in, swords drawn. But the rest of the spies? Panic mode. They spread fear through the camp like a virus, convincing the people that certain doom awaits.

And so?

Israel—who had seen **God's presence in ways no human ever had**—chose fear.

They chose **to believe their eyes over their God.**

---

genetic engineering, human corruption, and the dangers of unchecked scientific ambition. While Peretti does not explicitly label this creature as Anakim, the book's themes of giant, monstrous beings, genetic corruption, and pre-Flood allusions align with some interpretations of the biblical Nephilim/Anakim narratives. And fine, maybe *This Present Darkness* and *Piercing The Darkness* aren't about Anakim or Nephilim per se, but you'll never be able to convince me that wasn't exactly what he was describing and had in mind without explicitly saying so. It was implied. Don't judge me, I was twelve. You're the problem, not me. You suck, Frank. Why didn't you just come out and say it? You ruined my childhood. Kidding, you made it. Can we be best-friends now?

And that choice?

It bought them 40 more years in the desert.

Lessons from the Nephilim Encounter

What's the real takeaway here?

It's not just about Israel's failure. It's about **faith in the face of terrifying odds**.

Because here's the reality: every believer **is faced with Nephilim moments**—times when fear whispers, "This is too big. You can't win."

- The diagnosis that looks terminal.
- The financial ruin that seems irreversible.
- The cultural tide that feels unstoppable.

But Caleb and Joshua? They show us the way forward.

Faith doesn't ignore the giants. It **acknowledges them**—but refuses to **make them bigger than God**.

And that?

That is the secret to taking the land.

The Nephilim Sadness

When the spies report back, Israel collectively loses its mind.

"Would that we had died in Egypt!"

Translation: *At least in Egypt, we'd be killed by normal-sized humans!*

"Or would that we had died in this wilderness!"

God, overhearing this, is like, *"Oh, that's an option? Noted."*

"Why is the Lord bringing us into this land—to fall by the sword?"

Wait... is that what God's plan really leads to? Unending suffering? Pain stacked on pain?

Then comes the final gut punch:

"Would it not be better for us to go back to Egypt?"

Bro. No.

There's *nothing* left in Egypt. God systematically dismantled that entire civilization. It's a wasteland. No food. No jobs. No army. Their firstborns are dead. Their infrastructure is wrecked. You plundered their gold on the way out. If you try to walk back in there, they would 100% kill you on sight.

And yet, because of fear, they are *seriously* considering it.

Enter Joshua and Caleb

Moses and Aaron—fully aware that God is about to *Dracarys*[6] some fools—hit the deck, face down.

Joshua and Caleb see this and instantly panic. It's like when you're walking through the jungle, and suddenly your sergeant drops to the ground. You don't ask questions. You *drop too.*

Then, in a desperate bid to keep the people from making the single dumbest decision of their lives, Joshua and Caleb make one final plea:

> *"The land is exceedingly good! If the Lord delights in us, He will give it to us! Only do not rebel against the Lord!"*

Too late.

---

[6] I've never seen *GoT* because I'm a Christian and it's insulting that you would presume to think I would *ever* entertain myself with violence, gore, and nudity. Honestly, put this book down–I don't want you reading it anymore. Fine, I'll explain myself. I heard–from a pagan co-worker (ew, not my friend–would never)–that *dracarys* is the command given to the dragons to bring forth fire from their fire-guts, when an enemy needs to be turned to ash–if you must know.

The Real Enemy: Fear

Let's fast forward to Revelation 21:8.

You're coasting through the final victory lap of Scripture. Jesus is fixing everything. You're sipping wine by the fire, feeling good. And then, out of nowhere, you hit this list of people getting thrown into the lake of fire:

> *"The murderers (yup, dunk them), the sexually immoral (pedos—double dunk!), the liars (politicians—get 'em!), the sorcerers (Harry Potter? Toss 'em in!), and... cowards?"*

Wait. Cowards?!

No Bible, no! That hits different!

I struggle with fear! My Mom struggles with fear! My whole family could be cast in an anxiety-driven sitcom. We call my Mom *Debbie Downer* because she has an encyclopedic knowledge of how people die from *everything*.

She knows exactly which foods cause choking. She knows which weather conditions increase the likelihood of a car crash. She watches *plane crash documentaries the night before flying*.

Meanwhile, my younger brother Gabe? Absolute zero fear.

At theme parks, I'd be scheming ways to avoid rollercoasters. Gabe? First in line, hands up, screaming, *"Send it!"*

That's when I realized: **faith and fear define your future.**

Israel had literally seen the Red Sea split in half. They had witnessed divine power beyond human comprehension. And yet... one word—*Nephilim*—was enough to break them.

Fear rewrote their history. Fear hijacked their faith. Fear blinded them to reality.

So I have to ask: What is fear keeping *you* from?

Anxiety: The Life Saver

I once read that anxiety is like an evolutionary "fuel low" light blinking on your brain's dashboard—an internal warning system meant to help you make the right decision when danger looms.

Anxiety is *fear of future pain*—and sometimes, that's a *good* thing.

Let's say my brother Gabe and I are running around in the jungle when a saber-toothed tiger emerges from the brush. My brain immediately processes the situation: *I don't have a weapon, I'm a slow runner, and this is bad.*

My anxiety kicks in, screaming, *"Run, idiot, run!"* and I obey.

But Gabe? He has no fear. No hesitation. He attacks the tiger with nothing but a stick and a *gleam in his eye*. If I'm a betting man, I'm putting all my money on the tiger.

And just like that, Gabe is lunch.

His anxiety didn't kick in when it *should* have, and he paid the price.

This is what's happening in Numbers 13. The spies aren't *completely* wrong to be worried. They've done the math. They realize that, in *natural* terms, they *do not* have the firepower to take Canaan.

That's a fact. And facts *matter*.

Faith does *not* dismiss facts.

Anyone who tells you that faith is about *ignoring* facts is selling something.

The Real Problem: Forgetting Who's in Charge

The issue isn't *fear*—it's **who they think is responsible for winning the battle.**

The ten spies have forgotten how they got here. Somewhere along the way, they started believing that *they* were the ones who got themselves out of Egypt.

Moses has to correct this exact kind of thinking later in Deuteronomy 8:11, 17, saying:

> *"Take care lest you forget the Lord your God... who brought you out of the land of Egypt... lest you say in your heart, 'My power and the might of my hand have gotten me this wealth.'"*

But this is *exactly* the mentality of the ten spies:

> *"We got ourselves out of Egypt."*
> *"We have to take Canaan ourselves."*
> *"We don't have what it takes."*
> *"We're doomed."*

The Ultimate Irony: It Was Never Theirs to Take

The craziest part?

Canaan isn't even *theirs* to take.

It's **God's.**

God is the *landlord*. They're not *taking* Canaan; they're *receiving* it.

This isn't a game of military conquest. It's a *divine inheritance*.

God has already signed the deed over to them. Their job is to show up and take the keys.

And if it's *God's* idea, it's *God's* job to make it happen.

The old preachers used to say:

> *"If it's His will, it's His bill."*

And they were exactly right.

If *God* declared it, *God* will accomplish it.

But here we are, with so many Christians confused about how faith actually works.

We don't fight for victory.

We fight *from* victory.

But when we forget who actually wins the battle, fear takes over.

And suddenly?

The giants in the land start looking bigger than the God who made them.

Faith Begins With God

Faith isn't something that starts with us—it starts with God. That's critical. Because if faith were something we had to manufacture from scratch, we'd all be doomed.

Romans 10:17 says it plain as day:

"Faith comes by hearing, and hearing by the Word of Christ."

Faith isn't about manifesting your best life or scribbling down "dream boards" filled with yachts and six-pack abs. It's not positive vibes or Oprah-style visualization techniques. And it's definitely not just raw optimism with a sprinkle of spirituality.

Faith is responding to a real Person's real Word.

Abram didn't sit around in Ur of the Chaldees thinking, *You know what would be fun? Leaving everything I've ever known, wandering through the desert, and fathering an entirely new civilization at the age of 75.* That was not on his vision board.

No—**God spoke**. And Abram responded.

Faith doesn't require that you know all the details. It doesn't mean you get a divine blueprint emailed to you with all contingencies covered. It simply means you trust that **God knows** the details, and you have enough of His Word to take the next step.

That's where the ten spies went catastrophically wrong. The issue wasn't their fear. The issue wasn't even that they noticed the giants. **The issue was that they rejected God's Word altogether.**

The Real Meaning of "Cowardice"

Let's go back to Revelation 21:8 for a moment—the famous "lake of fire" verse. It includes a list of people who will receive eternal judgment:

> *"But as for the cowardly, the faithless, the detestable, as for murderers, the sexually immoral, sorcerers, idolaters, and all liars, their portion will be in the lake that burns with fire and sulfur, which is the second death."*

And suddenly, in the middle of this lineup of villains, there's an unexpected guest: **the cowardly.**

Wait—what?

God's eternal wrath isn't *burning hot* against people who don't like public speaking. He's not sending people to hell because they refuse to go skydiving.

No—**the cowardice in Revelation 21 refers to unfaithful witnesses.**

It's about people who **shrink back from following Christ** because of:

- The threat of persecution
- The cost of social rejection

- The fear of being unpopular
- The pressure of comfort and compromise

That's the cowardice that gets "rewarded" with fire.

And Joshua—standing in front of a trembling Israel—calls it out for what it is: **rebellion.**

In Numbers 14:9, Joshua doesn't say, *"Hey guys, let's try to be a little braver, okay?"* No—he says,

"Only do not rebel against the LORD. And do not be afraid of the people of the land, because we will devour them."

He **links** cowardice and rebellion.

And history shows exactly how this plays out. That entire faithless generation? They **die in the wilderness.** The very land they were afraid to enter? **It goes to their children instead.**

They literally chose the wilderness over the promise—and they got exactly what they wanted.

Fast forward centuries later, and the writer of **Hebrews issues the same warning to Jewish Christians:**

"Don't make the same mistake. Don't shrink back from Jesus."

It's like God is pleading: *Don't be like your ancestors. Don't die in a spiritual desert because you're afraid to trust Me.*

Learning Obedience vs. Rebellion

Now, before anyone panics—there's a huge difference between:

1. **Learning obedience**
2. **Rebelling against God**

They are **not** the same thing.

I'm learning obedience every single day.

I mess up in my worship, in my devotion, in my giving. I struggle in my faith, my boldness, my willingness to step out. Sometimes I hesitate. Sometimes I doubt. Sometimes I wake up and think, *God, I have no clue how to do this life thing.*

And **God is merciful, patient, and kind.**

"His mercies never fail—they are new every morning." (Lamentations 3:22-23)

That's not rebellion. That's **growth**.

Rebellion is different. Rebellion isn't wrestling with obedience—it's **rejecting** it.

- Learning obedience says, *"God, You're right—I'm wrong. Help me obey."*
- Rebellion says, *"God, Your Word is wrong. I don't trust it. I decide what's true."*

That's what got Israel killed in the wilderness.

That's what made them beg to go back to Egypt.

That's what kept them from **receiving** what was already theirs.

And that's what so many people today are caught up in.

They don't want to **learn** obedience.

They don't want to **wrestle** with Scripture.

They want to **rewrite** the Word of God to fit their desires.

And the moment you start reshaping Scripture to fit your will, instead of reshaping your will to fit Scripture?

You've already lost the battle.

A Crisis of Cowardice

We are in a full-scale crisis of cowardice in the Western Church. Not a mild downturn. Not a "let's tweak a few things and get back on track" situation. No—this is an all-out collapse of courage.

We know God calls us to raise our kids in the fear of the Lord. We read Proverbs 22:6 and nod our heads: *Train up a child in the way he should go, and when he is old, he will not depart from it.* But then? We ship them off to Egypt's school system, where they're catechized in secularism, drilled in gender theory, and trained to despise biblical morality. And we tell ourselves, *Well, we'll just take them to church on Sundays and hope for the best!*

Hope for the best? Are we serious? That's like sending your kid to a vegan camp for six months and expecting them to come home craving steak.

We justify it because Christian education seems too overwhelming. Too expensive. Too radical. We don't want to fight that Canaanite battle—it's a land too difficult to conquer. And so, we let the world disciple them. And we act shocked when, at the ripe old age of 18, they walk away from the faith, armed with an entire belief system that mocks everything we hold dear.

I see this everywhere I go—youth conferences, young adult events, retreats, summer camps. The crisis is massive. It's not a trickle of deconstruction; it's an avalanche of apostasy. The younger generation has been mentored by TikTok influencers, educated by the state, and shaped by online echo chambers of progressive idealism.

And now? They're rejecting biblical Christianity, sprinting into the arms of:

- Woke spirituality (*a weird hybrid of Buddhism, activism, and self-worship*)

- Empathy cults (*where "loving someone" means affirming every single bad idea they have*)
- Progressive apostasy disguised as "modern faith" (*which is just recycled heresy with better graphic design*)

Why? Because they fear the inhabitants of the land. They think the political Nephilim will rip their arms off and eat their heads. They believe that if they stand for biblical truth, the culture will devour them whole. And to be honest, they're not entirely wrong—the world is ruthless to those who dissent. But here's the thing: fear doesn't get the final say. Faith does.

The Church Is God's Bet

Let me be crystal clear: **Jesus is all in on the Church.**

Not kind of in. Not partially invested. **All in.**

He knows the future. He's not worried about cultural trends or social movements. He's not biting His nails over Gen Z deconstruction rates or the latest CNN headline.

He **knows** the Church will win.

He **knows** the Kingdom will advance.

He **knows** His Bride will be victorious.

And so, when we invest in the Church—when we give, serve, build, pray, evangelize, teach—we are putting our money where God's mouth is. We are saying, *God, I trust that You are telling the truth when You say the gates of hell will not prevail against Your Church (Matt. 16:18).*

That's what faith does. Faith doesn't hedge its bets. Faith doesn't place a side wager on secularism just in case biblical Christianity isn't "relevant" enough.

Faith believes. And because faith believes—**it speaks.**

So the question remains: **Will we be faithful witnesses?**

Or will we shrink back in fear?

Because faith says, *Let God be true and every man a liar* (Rom. 3:4).

Sharknado: When Fear Hijacks Reality

Let's talk about what happened with the ten spies.

These guys—let's call them the first-century CNN—really started to go off the rails when Joshua and Caleb pushed back. It wasn't enough that they saw giants; they had to escalate the story.

First, they claimed, *"The land devours its inhabitants."*

Really? The land just eats people? Is this quicksand on steroids?

Next, they said, *"All the people are tall."*

All of them? Every single one? Even the toddlers? Sounds unlikely.

And then, they hit peak hysteria:

> *"We looked like grasshoppers in their eyes!"*

Okay, now we're in full-blown fever dream mode.

Unbelief, as it turns out, has a wild imagination.

I've noticed this in my own life. When I'm in full-blown coward mode, the first thing to go isn't my dignity or my composure—it's my sense of proportion. Everything suddenly feels apocalyptic. A single critique turns into *"Everyone hates me."* A difficult season becomes *"I'm going to fail at life."* A minor setback morphs into *"God has abandoned me."*

None of what the ten spies said was actually true.

The land did not devour people.

Not everyone was a giant—just a select few.

And they did not look like grasshoppers.

At this point, fear had taken the wheel. They were catastrophizing like Dorothy and her traveling circus en route to Oz. Seeing things. Saying things. Utterly detached from reality.

It's the ancient equivalent of screaming, *"And we saw sharks with laser beams on their heads!"*

Cue mass hysteria.

The people lose it:

> *"Sharks with laser beams?! Oh great. Did you hear that, Ron? Now we've got sharks with laser beams on our hands."*

Someone asks, *"Wait, how did the sharks get on land?"*

One of the idiot spies, now fully committed to the fiction, blurts out, *"Because of... a... Sharknado. Yes—a tornado that has sharks in it! Spitting sharks everywhere!"*

And just like that, the entire camp goes into a full-blown meltdown.

Meanwhile, Joshua and Caleb—fully exhausted by the absolute nonsense they are hearing—roll their eyes.

> *"People—please. Please. Stop listening to these guys. They are liars. And cowards. There is no such thing as a Sharknado, and we don't even have the technology for laser beams yet. This is ridiculous."*

But it's too late.

The contagion of fear has spread. The masses have bought in. The lie has won the day.

The Tragic Irony of Fear

And here's the kicker: **the thing they feared the most happened because of their fear.**

They were afraid they would die in the wilderness?

God said, "Fine. You will."

They were afraid their children would be taken captive?

God said, "Actually, they're the ones who will inherit the land while you perish."

Their fear led to disobedience. Their disobedience led to judgment.

And this is what's happening today.

The Western Church, in many ways, has adopted the mindset of the ten spies.

We see the giants of secularism. We see the fortified walls of postmodernism. We see the Nephilim of academia, media, and culture.

And we panic.

We tell ourselves, *"It's too much. The culture war is lost. The Church is irrelevant. We're grasshoppers."*

And God is looking down, saying, *"Are you serious? Have you learned nothing? Did I not tell you the gates of hell will not prevail? Did I not promise to build My Church? Did I not guarantee My victory?"*

But for so many, fear wins out.

And just like that faithless generation in Numbers 14, many will choose the wilderness over the promise.

But not Joshua.

Not Caleb.

Not the fearless remnant.

Because God is raising up a different kind of Church in these last days.

A Church that doesn't bow.

A Church that doesn't shrink back.

A Church that refuses to buy into the lie of the Sharknado.

A Church that actually believes God's Word.

The Joshua Church

The Joshua Church believes God's word and refuses to collapse under the weight of its own insecurities. It practices faith in the face of legitimate obstacles—real giants, real barriers, real opposition. It does not pretend the enemies aren't there. It does not downplay the difficulties. But it also does not manufacture Sharknados.

The Joshua Church is not naive. It does not march blindly into battle, assuming victory based on good vibes and sheer optimism. It marches because God has spoken. It recognizes that the Promised Land is impossible to attain in its own strength. But that's the whole point. If it were doable, God wouldn't have been involved in the first place. The conquest is supernatural, and the victory is God's.

The Joshua Church operates on God's idea—which means the conquest will happen on God's terms, in God's timing, and with God's power. This requires radical trust and unwavering obedience. It is not a church of cautious diplomats, hedging their bets. It is not a church of half-believers, waiting to see which way the cultural winds will blow. It is a church with one foot in the Jordan, ready to cross before the waters part.

It is a church that understands the assignment. A church that doesn't need God to hand them blueprints with contingencies, financial projections, and strategic outcomes before they take the first step. The Joshua Church doesn't wait until the coast is clear—it moves because faith is a verb. It believes that the walls don't fall before the march, but because of it.

And crucially, the Joshua Church requires corporate solidarity. There cannot be a "mixed multitude" in the congregation—no coalition of half-hearted believers moonlighting as disciples, no spiritual tourists looking for a temporary fix, no lukewarm spectators playing at devotion while clutching their exit strategies. It must be an all-in generation, a church carrying the weight of faith together. A church with one voice, one vision, and one unwavering conviction: If God is for us, who can be against us?

After Moses dies, Joshua takes command. The first city on the list? Jericho.

Having learned his lesson from the wilderness debacle, Joshua doesn't send twelve spies this time. He sends two. Because faith is not a democracy. It is not about polling opinions. Joshua doesn't need another round of fearful men running the numbers and freaking out. He needs a faithful witness.

No doubt, the two witnesses in Revelation symbolize this same idea: a Faithful Church. Two men who, despite the absurd strength of the city before them, are unshaken. They know that if God said Jericho was theirs, then Jericho was already a done deal.

And when the battle begins, Joshua fights it God's way—a test of his faithfulness to the Word.

A week-long march. A silent procession. A final, thunderous shout.

And what happens?

The walls come down.

Not because of military genius. Not because of superior firepower. Not because of a strategic assault with battering rams. Not because of cunning political maneuvering or grassroots activism.

The walls fall because faith is obedience in motion.

The Joshua Church marches, shouts, and watches God do what only He can do. It does not rely on human ingenuity, but divine certainty. It does not operate by worldly logic, but by supernatural truth.

It is the Church that understands: Victory does not come by the strength of its hands, but by the faithfulness of its heart. And that is why the Joshua Church will always stand victorious—because it is never standing alone.

Chapter Six

The Elijah Church

During the time of the Kings, Israel—the Northern Kingdom—had Samaria as its capital, while Judah, the Southern Kingdom, remained centered in Jerusalem.

The kingdom had fractured after Solomon's son, Rehoboam, made what could only be described as a historically bad decision: doubling down on oppression when his advisors begged him to lighten up. This set off a rebellion, led by Jeroboam (a man with an almost identical name, just to keep things confusing), who convinced the northern tribes to sever ties with the House of David and resist the southern monarchy.

Jeroboam, realizing it would be a major political problem if his people kept traveling down to Jerusalem (in Judah) to worship, concocted a hybrid religion—half YHWH, half idolatry—ensuring his newly minted kingdom's total independence. The result? Spiritual and political apostasy on a national scale.

And God was, as you might imagine, not thrilled.

So, He sent prophets to warn the kings of Israel that their half-and-half theology wasn't just doctrinally unsound—it was existentially dangerous. The land they occupied did not belong to them; it belonged to YHWH. If they refused to realign with Him, He would evict them like a divine landlord with a heavenly eviction notice.

Enter Elijah, whose very name—**YHWH is El**—functioned as both a theological statement and a political act of defiance. "El" was a generic term for "god" in the Canaanite pantheon, and Elijah's name made it unmistakably clear: the real El wasn't Baal, wasn't Asherah, wasn't any of the knockoff deities floating around the ancient Near East. The true El was YHWH.

And Elijah had arrived to make that known.

Elijah vs. Ahab and Jezebel: The Battle for Israel's Soul

Elijah's ministry unfolded during Israel's peak apostasy. Omri, Israel's king, had brokered a political and economic alliance with the Phoenicians—one of the wealthiest maritime powers of the Mediterranean. With their trade fleets and economic influence, Israel was about to hit a serious financial windfall. Prosperity meant power. Power meant self-reliance. And self-reliance meant YHWH was no longer necessary.

To seal the deal, Omri arranged for his son, Ahab, to marry Jezebel, the daughter of Ethbaal, the Tyrian king-priest.

Jezebel wasn't just royalty—she was a **priestess** of the Tyrian Baal, and she came fully prepared to remake Israel in Baal's image. Upon arrival, she didn't just suggest Baal worship; **she institutionalized it.** She established 450 state-sponsored prophets of Baal, along with 400 prophets of Asherah, turning state religion into a political weapon.

And the result? Baal worship became the national religion, fully subsidized by the monarchy.

This wasn't just **a little idolatry on the side.** This was **Baalism on steroids.** Government-funded. Politically enforced. A wholesale rebranding of Israel's spiritual identity.

Elijah's School of the Prophets, therefore, wasn't just a theological institution—it was **a countercultural resistance movement.** Jezebel wasn't content with merely pushing Baal; she actively hunted the prophets of YHWH, financing schools that indoctrinated Israel's youth into state-sanctioned apostasy.

So YHWH, in response to Israel's arrogance, **shut off the rain.**
In an agrarian society where Israel's primary export to Phoenicia was crops, this was **a total economic nuke.** Jezebel's entire financial bet on Baal's fertility cult was now **bankrupt.** The god she had imported—the rain god, the fertility god, the prosperity god—couldn't make it drizzle.

Elijah was sent to remind Ahab exactly **who ran the weather.**

The Hard Word

Elijah's ministry was **the hard word.**

When comparing Elijah and Elisha, it's impossible not to notice the pattern: **Elijah was the bad cop; Elisha, the good cop.** Elijah's words were judgment; Elisha's words were restoration.

This wasn't about **personality**—it was about **context.**

Elijah was called to rebuke a nation in active rebellion—to announce **disaster before deliverance.** Elisha, on the other hand, ministered in a season of renewal and rebuilding.

Luke picks up on this theme in his Gospel and the book of Acts. He frames **Jesus as the new Elijah**—a prophet sent to **indict the religious and political elite**—and then frames the Holy Spirit as **Elisha,** sent to restore and empower the people of God.

Jesus's ministry, like Elijah's, was not well received. His first sermon in His hometown nearly got Him thrown off a cliff. His parables weren't **comforting morality tales**; they were **blunt-force warnings about impending disaster.**

"You are running out of time. Repent now."

And the **Elijah Church** is the Church given this ministry—to call **rebellious empires back to repentance.**

This is not the mission of the Elisha Church—**which comforts the broken, restores the faithful, and builds in peacetime.**

No—**the Elijah Church is war-time.**

The Elijah Church preaches in Nineveh **before the city repents.**

The Elijah Church speaks in Babylon **while Nebuchadnezzar still believes he's a god.**

The Elijah Church stands before Ahab and Jezebel **while the prophets of Baal are still on salary.**

And what does it say?

It says the hard thing.

The thing that will get it canceled.

The thing that will get it censored.

The thing that might get it killed.

Because when Jezebel runs the theological seminaries, when state religion is a **paganized, government-funded, zealously enforced ideology,** the Elijah Church doesn't just "engage in conversation."

The Elijah Church **plants Schools of the Prophets.**

It creates **an alternative theological education** for the next generation of preachers, pastors, and leaders. It builds parallel institutions. It refuses to **play by the empire's rules.**

Or as my friend Jon Norman, pastor of Soul Church in the UK, puts it:

Plant a school, not a campus.

This is not the era of **"seeker-sensitive, inoffensive, play-nice" Christianity.**

This is **Elijah's era.**

Ahab is on the throne.

Jezebel is running the cultural institutions.

Baal is the state religion.

The false prophets are **the thought leaders of the empire.**

And yet, the true prophets **are still here.**

God **always** reserves a remnant.

And in the days of Elijah, **that remnant was hidden in caves.**

But not forever.

Because Elijah is about to walk into Ahab's palace, point his finger at the king, and say:

"It will not rain except at my word."

And that?

That is what the Elijah Church does.

It **shuts down** the false gods of the age.

It **speaks the hard word.**

And it **calls an empire to repentance.**

This is the Church the world needs now.

This is **the Elijah Church.**

The Elijah Church in the Age of Apostasy

We live in an era of **active** apostasy.

Not casual drifting. Not mild disinterest. Not the kind of "I don't really believe in God, but Christmas music still slaps" agnosticism. No—this is **full-scale, organized rebellion** against the God of Scripture.

Our educational institutions? They have been repurposed as **state-run theological seminaries**—not for Christianity, but for the new Secularist Theocracy, the established and unquestionable dogma of the age. Every child that enters these institutions gets baptized—not in water, but in **a worldview that declares man his own god, morality a social construct, and truth an oppressive relic of a bygone age.**

This isn't passive. This isn't accidental. This is **Jezebel's regime in full force.**

Every Church that recognizes this as a spiritual war—every Church that **refuses to send its kids to Jezebel's catechism classes**—every Church that builds alternative education systems, from homeschool co-ops to Bible-rooted universities—**is stepping into the prophetic mantle of Elijah.**

And make no mistake: **The Elijah Church is hated.**

It is blacklisted. It is mocked. It is deplatformed. It is cast as the villain of the cultural narrative. And why? Because it refuses to kneel.

The Elijah Church does not care about mass appeal.

It does not spend its days begging for cultural approval, neutering its sermons to avoid offending TikTok theologians, or adjusting its worship to sound more like a Spotify playlist. **It is not trying to "reach" the world by becoming the world.**

It is **a hunted assembly, a remnant in exile, an immovable rock standing in defiance against the floodwaters of apostasy.**

And yet, **it is this Church—this stubborn, unshakable Church—that carries the seed of national renewal.**

Because **Elisha does not come before Elijah.**

Restoration does not come before judgment.

And until the lies are exposed, until a prophet stands and points to the sky and says, "It will not rain until God says so," until someone shatters the illusion of self-sufficiency, **the people will remain enslaved to the empire.**

This is why the Elijah Church exists.

The Elijah Meltdown

Elijah is, to put it mildly, **an absolute mess.**

And this is **not** the sanitized, flannel-graph[7] version of Elijah—the one where he just goes around leveling false prophets with a

---

[7] Some of you Gen-Z kids don't know what a flannel graph board is and that's because your parents don't love you. Think Velcro-meets-chalk-board—you can stick soft cloth figures on a background, like Moses and Aaron walking through a wilderness. It's literally how us Millennials learned everything about the Bible as kids. We didn't grow up with iPads, that's why we still have brains while you vegetables drool over quasi-educational catfish.

holy scowl. No, Elijah is **one of the most psychologically volatile figures in Scripture.**

If **David is the hot-headed warrior-poet,** and **Jeremiah is the tortured emo-prophet,** then **Elijah is the burnout who goes from total triumph to total despair in five minutes.**

Paul Kissling suggests that the original audience of 1 Kings would have seen Elijah as a **stoic, unshakable force of nature—** up until chapter 17. **Then, the breakdown starts.** Then, the emotional cracks begin to widen.

James (5:17) goes so far as to say that Elijah was "a man with a nature like ours." Translation? **Elijah was unstable. Elijah was human. Elijah was—let's be real—kind of a disaster.**

And nowhere is this more obvious than at the **absolute peak** of his ministry.

Let's set the scene: **Elijah has just humiliated 450 prophets of Baal in the biggest divine flex in Old Testament history.**

He didn't just **defeat** them—he **roasted them.**

At first, it was just mild banter—"Maybe Baal is sleeping? Maybe he's taking a long trip?"—but by the end, Elijah was **mocking them with the prophetic equivalent of a Twitter dunk contest.**

Then, after they spent hours **cutting themselves and wailing like lunatics,** Elijah steps forward, **soaks the altar in water,** and calls on YHWH.

Fire falls. The altar is obliterated. The people collapse in awe.

And then?

Elijah has **every last prophet of Baal dragged down to the Kishon Valley and executed on the spot.**

It's a defining moment. A resounding victory. A triumph for the ages.

And yet…

Immediately after, Elijah collapses into a nervous break-down and quits the ministry.

The Prophet Who Buckled

Elijah **didn't just doubt. He didn't just waver.**
He straight-up quit.
This wasn't a brief moment of weakness, a fleeting question of faith. No—**this was a full-blown existential crisis, a ministerial burnout of apocalyptic proportions.**
He had just **witnessed the fire of God descend from heaven.** He had **absolute proof that YHWH was the one true God.** He had **experienced supernatural vindication on a level that would make Moses jealous.**
And yet, **as soon as he hears Jezebel wants him dead, he bolts.**
Think about this for a second. **Jezebel had already been trying to kill him.** For years.
Why did this particular death threat send him spiraling into despair?
A real prophet would have stood his ground, right? A real man of God would have **doubled down,** ridden the momentum of victory, stormed the palace, and **ripped Jezebel's pagan shrines to the ground.**
But that's not what happens.
Elijah **quits.**
He fires his servant.
He runs into the desert.
He collapses under a broom tree and begs God to kill him.
"Just end it now, Lord. I'm done."
The sheer irony of **winning the biggest fight of his life and then immediately losing the will to live** isn't lost on the reader.

If this were a stage play, the audience would be cackling at the absurdity of it all.

It's like watching a superhero movie where the hero defeats the villain, saves the world, and then five minutes later has **a total breakdown over an overdue parking ticket.**

The Elijah Church Will Burn Out

I've watched **a lot** of Elijah Churches have their own **meltdowns.**

Especially in 2020.

Good, godly leaders—men and women who had been **absolute rocks** in the faith—suddenly **buckled under the weight of the moment.**

Not because they didn't know the truth.

Not because they lacked conviction.

But because **the cost of standing firm suddenly felt unbearable.**

I watched pastors **cave to the Covid cult,** parroting whatever state-sponsored nonsense they were fed on CNN.

I watched leaders **bend the knee to the BLM mob,** adopting a secular racial theology that had more in common with Marx than Matthew.

I watched churches **comply with every tyrannical demand of the empire,** all while preaching sermons on how we should "submit to authorities"—as if the authorities were somehow above God.

And now?

The receipts are in.

We've since learned that **Progressivism is a societal death spiral** in every nation that tolerates it.

We've since learned that **the vaccine was a farce**—meaning every "moral imperative" speech was built on lies.

We've since learned that **Black Lives Matter was a literal Marxist scam**—a political grift designed to fleece corporations and destabilize cities.

And yet, **when it mattered,** the Elijah Churches **wilted.**

They **ran into the wilderness.**

They **collapsed under the broom tree.**

They **begged for an easy way out.**

This is what happens when we think **winning the battle means the war is over.**

This is what happens when **we think victory should make things easier.**

Elijah won the greatest fight of his life—**and then reality hit.**

The work wasn't done.

The war wasn't over.

And the Elijah Church—if it is to survive—**must prepare for what comes after the fire falls.**

The 2020 Elijah Churches

I watched a lot of Elijah Churches have their own meltdowns in 2020. Not just minor existential crises, but full-scale, panic-room, "break the glass and hit the eject button" style implosions. Churches that had stood tall for decades, preaching about courage and the sovereignty of God, suddenly began speaking in the hushed, calculated tones of corporate HR departments, issuing statements that sounded like they were penned by interns at BuzzFeed.

Good, godly men and women—faithful pastors who had been rock solid for years—lost the plot. They didn't even put up a fight. It wasn't that they suddenly became raging heretics. It wasn't that they abandoned the gospel for a golden calf of hedonism and personal wealth (that would've at least been interesting). No, they simply folded under pressure, wilted under the cultural heat lamp, and let the world dictate their theological convictions.

They got spooked by the election drama, and **the nation paid the price.**

They got spooked by the Covid Inquisitors, and **their congregations paid the price.**

They got spooked by the Black Lives Matter Mafia, and their people were left **confused and divided** because they were confused and divided.

And now? Now, with the benefit of hindsight, we can see what happened with crystal clarity: they let fear make their decisions for them. They outsourced their moral compass to Twitter polls and blue-check activist grifters who have since moved on to their next hustle. We have learned—though they have not—that Progressivism is not a gentle social correction but a theological wrecking ball. Wherever it goes, it doesn't just "reform" or "modernize"—it razes, hollows out, and leaves behind a nihilistic wasteland where meaning once stood.

We've learned that the pandemic wasn't just a health crisis—it was a compliance test. And much of the Church failed it. We've learned that BLM wasn't some grassroots push for racial unity but a tax-exempt laundering operation for Marxist revolutionaries. And yet, during the meltdown, mainstream Evangelicalism & Co. didn't just nod along—they baptized it, sanctified it, and wove it into their sermons like it was a fresh revelation from Sinai.

Historic Christian thinkers would have laughed them out of the room.

Augustine? Would have torched it with **rhetorical napalm**.

Aquinas? Would have shredded it with **logic**.

Luther? Would have **mocked it** in German so hard it would still be echoing in the halls of Wittenberg.

Calvin? Would have dismissed it as the **deranged delusions of men who never read their Bibles.**

Wesley? Would have called it a work of **Satan himself.**

Chesterton? Would have written a scathing essay **exposing its incoherence.**

Lewis? Would have **eviscerated** its moral cowardice with surgical precision.

But today's Evangelical theologians?

They're politically impoverished because they don't think historically. They believe they are forging a new and enlightened path, bravely confronting *"the sins of the Church"* with a level of self-awareness never before seen. But in reality, they are simply repackaging yesterday's errors with today's hashtags. They have no sense of continuity. They see themselves as Odysseus on his way home to Ithaca, navigating new intellectual terrain with great wisdom and care. When in reality, they are just Odysseus on his way to Troy, marching headfirst into a battle they do not understand, completely unaware that their so-called progress is a regression into chaos.

They cannot read Lewis because he exposes their cultural biases. He believed in just deserts and opposed women in the priesthood—so he is discarded.

They quote Chesterton, but they cannot stomach him. He dismantles their Postmodern instincts with his belief in tradition—what he called *"the democracy of the dead."*

They dismiss Calvin because he burned heretics, but they fully embrace the secularists who burn dissenters on the altar of political correctness.

They admire Aquinas and Augustine, but they ignore their political realism, their just war theory, their common-sense approach to borders, law, and national sovereignty.

Modern Evangelicalism, in short, hates the idea of a Nation. It cannot conceptualize the idea that the Church is not merely a set of personal beliefs but an institution that should **shape civilizations**. So it defaults to either Imperialism (let the globalist elites run everything and keep our heads down) or Tribalism (let's just form our own cozy subcultures and stop engaging at all), neither of which can sustain a free people.

It wants God to be a woman.

It wants the Church to retreat from the public square.

It wants the sexually deviant to be affirmed and gender binaries to be erased.

This is the spirit of the age. And the spirit of the age is never friendly to the Church. It is a parasite, and it always, always eats its host.

War Is Upon Us

Protestantism is in an *existential war*, and the war has **escalated**.

The choices before us are clear:

1. **Radically accept** the *thought-du-jour*. Become a Church of political trends, a willing servant of Jezebel's empire, a religious institution that exists to bless the latest madness.
2. **Radically reject** the *thought-du-jour*. Become a Church of historic substance, a faithful witness in *defiance* of the age.

And here's the thing:

You don't have to do *anything* to become a Jezebel robot.

Just send your kids to **public school**, read **mainstream media**, absorb **Hollywood's narratives**, agree with **corporate-sponsored activism**, nod along with **progressive academia**, and—voilà!— you will become a **perfectly programmed servant of the empire**.

Your theological instincts will be shaped entirely by the **state religion** of the age. And when you read Scripture through *that* lens, you will find a way to make it say **whatever you want**.

Biblical Literacy Isn't Enough

This is why *reading* the Bible isn't enough.

You need to be **transformed** by it.

You need **historic guides**—faithful men and women who read it rightly *before* us. You need the voices of the past—the Athanasiuses and Augustines, the Luthers and Calvins, the Wesleys and Spurgeons—to remind you that **truth is not dictated by the moment** but is tethered to eternity.

It takes *effort* to resist the tide.

- You have to seek out **alternative sources**.
- You have to read **old books** and study **old commentaries**.
- You have to **guard your words** in public spaces.
- You have to **speak in code** in certain company.
- You have to become a **Bible smuggler**—sometimes *inside your own church*.

And that's where the **anxiety** comes from.

Many pastors **never signed up for this fight**. They got into church leadership because they wanted to **lead**—not wage *war*.

But war is here, whether they like it or not.

The Courage to Stand

At *least* Elijah picked the fight.

Yes, he **buckled**.

Yes, he **panicked**.

Yes, he **ran**.

But at least he **engaged**.

Today, we don't need **strategic leaders** who hedge their bets and calculate the **risk-to-reward ratio** of telling the truth.

We don't need **Jimmy Carter**.

We need **Winston Churchill**.[8]

We need prophets and priests, not corporate managers **trying to keep everyone happy** while the walls of Christendom are being looted by activists, bureaucrats, and cowardly bishops.

And the good news?

The remnant is rising.

The Elijah Church vs. Jezebel's Robots

A friend of mine, a **Black pastor in New York City**, initially embraced the **George Floyd marches**. His church, like many others, found itself swept up in the fervor, with a number of **young women leading the charge**, recruiting church members to join in. His staff let it happen.

At first, it seemed like a moment of **unity**, a chance to **stand for justice**.

But the activism quickly metastasized into something else entirely—**Intersectionality Inc.**

As many of us who did our homework on **BLM** quickly realized (thanks to their conveniently public **mission statement** on their website), the movement wasn't *just* about racial justice. It was a **trojan horse** for a smorgasbord of ideological commitments—

- **Trans rights activism**
- **Queer theory**
- **Radical feminism**

---

[8] War is coming and the leadership of churches and governments will begin to shift, not because we want or desire it, but because in the absence of leadership, great decay has happened, and Progressives are militant—particularly Marxists. The survivors will be led by Churchill types—courageous, brave, and unwavering.

- **Anti-capitalism**
- **Anti-nuclear-family rhetoric**

And when these young women in his church **began hanging out with other activists**, they started **mainlining the full cocktail**.

Suddenly, it wasn't enough to be against **police brutality**—you had to be against **police departments existing at all**.

It wasn't enough to want **fair treatment**—you had to embrace **state-controlled wealth redistribution** and **economic dismantling**.

And if you *didn't* get on board?

You weren't just **indifferent**—you were a **bigot**.

Then came the **inevitable fallout**.

The women **left the church**, taking others with them, branding the pastor a **racist**, declaring that the leadership *"didn't care about justice."*

Because, of course—if you don't want to **dismantle the economy**, you're a **white supremacist**.

And this?

This is the **Jezebel Program** in action.

The Cycle of Crisis and Compliance

This won't be the last socio-political upheaval to test the Church. If anything, the tests are only getting harder. **Every generation faces its reckoning.** Some rise to the challenge, standing as faithful witnesses amid cultural collapse. Others cave faster than a cheap folding chair under a linebacker.

Everything is escalating. War and peace are cyclical. The people who don't read history think everything is getting progressively better because their college professors told them so. **But the rest**

of us? We know better. We can see the trajectory. If history teaches us anything, it's that empires always decay before they collapse. And once you reach the point where men in dresses are declaring themselves pregnant and entire government agencies are devoted to regulating speech, you've entered late-stage empire.

So the real question is this:

Will the Church buckle under pressure, like the German Church that traded its prophetic voice for state approval under the Third Reich? Or will there be an Elijah Church—a prophetic minority that refuses to compromise, refuses to surrender, and refuses to go along with the insanity of the moment?

Jezebel and the Puppet Administration

The anxiety that gripped Elijah wasn't just about Ahab—the guy with the official title. It was about **Jezebel**—the one actually pulling the strings. And this is where people get confused.

The empire's public face is almost never the one in charge. **Ahab was a placeholder. Jezebel was the power.** If you're looking at a president, prime minister, or chancellor and thinking, "This is the one making all the decisions," you don't understand how power works. **There is always a deeper network.** The handlers. The financiers. The ideologues shaping the narrative. The ones you don't see in the press conferences.

Jezebel is the picture of what happens when power and spiritual corruption become **one flesh.** And once that happens, it is incredibly difficult to untangle.

And here's the key: **Jezebel doesn't just rule. She re-educates.** She doesn't want to just silence the truth—she wants to replace it. The Northern Kingdom wasn't told to stop worshipping YHWH; they were told to integrate Baal into their theology. To blend. To compromise. To make peace with the regime by mixing in just enough state-approved ideology to avoid persecution.

That's the game plan today.

Jezebel doesn't need the Church to stop worshipping Christ. She just needs the Church to incorporate a little bit of the empire's religion into its doctrine. A little bit of woke. A little bit of "justice." A little bit of critical theory. A little bit of progressive theology. A little bit of "God is actually non-binary, and Jesus was a brown-skinned Palestinian activist."

Before you know it? **You've got Baal worship, but with crosses on the walls.**

Post-Disneyland Depression

After Elijah flees, quits the ministry, and begs God to kill him, something curious happens.

God doesn't rebuke him.

God doesn't lecture him.

God sends an angel. And the angel bakes him a cake.

This is one of the funniest, most bizarre moments in Scripture. Elijah collapses under a tree in full existential despair, and God's response? **Divine carbs.** He gives him cake and tells him to nap.

Elijah wakes up, eats the angel food, and then—like a teenager on summer break—goes straight back to bed.

Disneyland and the Crash

I once bought a Disneyland annual pass—the highest package, no blackout dates, no restrictions. **Pure, unfiltered magic, all year long.** I lived twenty minutes from the park, so I went **weekly,** sometimes just for fireworks or a late-night ride on Pirates of the Caribbean.

But by the time I got home? **Depression.**

Every time.

It's called **post-Disneyland depression.** You've just spent the entire day living in a fantasy world, stuffing your face with Mickey-shaped pretzels, dodging screaming toddlers in strollers, experiencing thrills and nostalgia in equal measure. You've walked through galaxies, sailed with buccaneers, and taken a harrowing journey through a haunted mansion.

And then?

You get in your Toyota Corolla, sit in L.A. traffic, and come home to bills, emails, and the sudden realization that your fridge is empty except for an expired tub of Greek yogurt. **Reality slaps you in the face.**

That's Elijah.

He went from calling down fire from heaven to hiding in a cave. From supernatural victory to wanting to die overnight.

From **lion to housecat.** From **bold warrior to man curled up in a fetal position, stress-eating angel cake.**

God's Reminder: It's Not Your Battle

What did Elijah need in that moment?

He needed to be reminded that the battle was never his to win.

Elijah's error wasn't that he confronted Jezebel—it was that he thought it was his job to defeat her.

This is where we get in trouble, too.

The Elijah Church is called to **confront** evil—political evil, cultural evil, spiritual evil. But we are not called to bear the weight of winning the whole war. **That's God's job.**

That's why the angel doesn't give Elijah a battle strategy. He gives him a nap and a snack. Because sometimes, **before God gives you a mission, He gives you a meal.**

The Myth of "Let Them Figure It Out"

This is where modern Evangelicalism loses the plot.

A lot of pastors don't want to **name** cultural evils. They want to "just preach Jesus" and "let people figure it out on their own."

That sounds nice in theory. It **feels** diplomatic. But it's also **nonsense.**

Paul didn't just "let them figure it out." He **wrote entire letters** calling out theological and cultural madness.

The Corinthians? The most "Spirit-filled" Church in the New Testament? They were also an absolute dumpster fire of sexual confusion.

Did Paul assume that just because they had "met Jesus" they'd automatically course-correct?

No.

He had to **call them out.**

Evangelical Leaders: Name the Thing

This is where modern pastors fail.

They don't want to **name the thing.**

They lead people to Jesus, and then their converts turn around and:

—Lobby for abortion.

—March for Marxist justice.

—Campaign for Drag Queen Story Hour.

—Advocate for transgender surgeries on minors.

That's not discipleship.

That's Jezebel's programming.

And if the Church doesn't **actively name** these things, we are just leaving people to be discipled by the empire.

Historic Christianity Had No Room for Jezebel

If you actually read the early Church Fathers, you'll notice something **blisteringly obvious**:

They didn't tolerate this kind of nonsense.

They had **zero** patience for people who wanted to mix Christianity with the reigning ideologies of the day.

They understood **exactly** what compromise looked like.

And yet today, the Church is so soft, so eager to be "relatable" and "winsome," that we are **tolerating things that 2,000 years of Christian history has always known were irredeemably wicked.**

What would Augustine say? He'd take a verbal flamethrower to half of modern Evangelicalism.

What would Luther do? Probably write an entire book eviscerating modern Christian cowardice, then slam it onto a church door.

What would Lewis say? He'd gut this soft, squishy theology with a single essay and leave people's heads spinning for decades.

We are not the first generation to deal with cultural insanity. The difference?

Past generations actually had the guts to fight it.

The Elijah Church Builds Schools, Not Campuses

The **Elijah Church** doesn't just **call out Jezebel**—it **creates an alternative**.

The key distinction between **Jezebel's prophets** and **Elijah's prophets** was **education**.

Jezebel's prophets were **trained in her state-funded religious schools**.

Elijah's prophets were **trained in underground schools of the Spirit**.

Jezebel was **committed to mass producing her disciples**.

Elijah was **committed to mass producing God's disciples**.

Which brings us to the crisis of the modern Church.

- We have **more churches than ever**—but **fewer schools than ever**.
- We have **bigger conferences**—but **weaker theological formation**.
- We have **massive campuses**—but **shrinking conviction**.

Jezebel is schooling an entire generation in her worldview.

And most of the Church?

Is **too afraid** to build an alternative.

The Call of the Elijah Church

The Elijah Church doesn't **just name the enemy**.

It **educates its people in the truth**.

It doesn't just **preach the Gospel**—it **forms disciples who know how to withstand Jezebel's empire**.

The question is:

Will we **build the schools of the prophets**?

Or will we let **Jezebel educate the next generation**?

The future of the Church depends on the answer.

Chapter Seven

The Pancake Church

In times of economic disaster, fortunes aren't annihilated so much as they are **re-shuffled, redistributed, and quietly reassigned**—like a rigged game of Monopoly where the guy who owns Boardwalk and Park Place suddenly offers up a trade no sane person would take, except that he's holding a rubber band to the back of your neck–I'd rather it be a revolver.

The smart investors—the ones playing chess while the rest of the world is busy knocking over checkers pieces in a panic—know this. They don't just survive chaos; they **salivate** over it. Because while everyone else is stuffing their cash under a mattress and stress-eating Cinnamon Toast Crunch, they're buying up everything in sight. **Opportunity doesn't die in crisis—it multiplies.**

And if you don't believe me, take a look at the Bible.

Pharaoh, Joseph, and the Greatest Real Estate Scam in History

When the seven-year famine hit the Middle East, Pharaoh didn't just survive the crisis—he **became a god.**

Here's how it went down:

- **Year One:** People still had money, so they used it to buy grain. Simple transactions.
- **Year Two:** The money ran dry. No problem. They sold their livestock.

- **Year Three:** Cattle gone. Time to sign over the **family land.**
- **Year Four: Whoops! No money, no livestock, no land.** So they did the only thing left. They sold **themselves** into servitude.

And just like that, Pharaoh became the legal owner of **everything. The famine didn't break his empire—it cemented it.** Every temple, every pyramid, every monument erected in his name? **Hard times real estate, baby.**

Joseph saw it coming. He warned Pharaoh in advance. And because of **one man's prophetic foresight**, Egypt became the world's food bank, loan shark, and government mortgage lender all in one.

And the most fascinating part? **The Egyptians were thankful.**

They didn't storm Pharaoh's palace with pitchforks and torches. They **expressed gratitude** for the very system that had enslaved them.

Because survival is survival. And when you're starving, you'll trade your last scrap of autonomy for a bowl of soup and **thank the man who gives it to you.**

And God? He was orchestrating all of it.

God Uses Storms to Move His People

Famine, drought, war—none of these things happen in a theological vacuum.

When the world descends into chaos, when nations implode under the weight of their own arrogance, when food disappears and economies collapse, it's not random. **It's a chess move.**

God uses catastrophe to shift the landscape.

He used the seven-year famine to **relocate** Jacob's family to Egypt—the only place where they could grow into a mighty nation.

He used **their eventual slavery** to push them **out** at the appointed time.

He used **Babylon's conquest** to purge Israel of its idolatry.

He used **Rome's brutality** to set the stage for the Gospel's explosion across the known world.

This is what people don't get about **divine judgment**.

It's never **just punishment**—it's **strategic.**

And that's what brings us to Elijah.

Phoenician Pancakes and the Hard Word

A famine had hit the land.

And now we have a problem.

Because while judgment is necessary, while the system must be reset, while evil must be confronted—**what happens to God's people in the middle of the crisis?**

What about the prophets? The faithful witnesses? The ones tasked with **delivering the inconvenient truths** in a world under divine reckoning?

Do they starve with everyone else?

Apparently not. Because while Israel is withering, Elijah is about to eat pancakes.

The Most Offensive Sermon in Nazareth's History

Fast forward to **Luke 4**, and Jesus is giving His first hometown sermon.

It does not go well.

At first, it's all good vibes. He reads from Isaiah, closes the scroll, sits down, and drops a **mic-level announcement:**

"This prophecy? Yeah. Just got fulfilled. By me."

Nazareth isn't sure what to do with that. **They start squinting.**

"Wait. Isn't this Joseph's son?"

Jesus, sensing the **low-key hostility**, does what any good preacher does when his audience is skeptical: **He makes it worse.**

"No prophet is accepted in his hometown."

Then He **really** goes for it:

"There were many widows in Israel in Elijah's time, when a severe famine struck the land.

But Elijah wasn't sent to any of them.

He was sent to a widow in **Zarephath, in the land of Sidon."**

Hold up. **Sidon?**

Phoenicia?

Jezebel's homeland?

What was Elijah—**Israel's top prophet, YHWH's mouthpiece, the Old Testament equivalent of a nuclear warhead—** doing **in the very land that helped lead Israel into apostasy?**

This is **why Nazareth lost their minds.**

Jesus wasn't just reminding them of Elijah's journey—**He was making a point.**

Israel was experiencing a **spiritual famine** in Jesus' day.

And just like in Elijah's day, **God wasn't feeding His prophets in Israel.**

He was feeding them **somewhere else.**

And that's when the hometown crowd **turns into a lynch mob.**

They try to **throw Him off a cliff.**

Because nothing enrages **religious people** more than the realization that God isn't exclusively on their side.

The Elijah Church and the Pancake Principle

This is the brutal reality of prophetic ministry.

If you think the system is corrupt—God thinks it's more corrupt than you do.

If you think judgment is coming—**God has already packed His prophet a suitcase and sent him on a one-way trip to Sidon.**

And the **Elijah Church?**

The one that calls out cultural evil?

The one that refuses to play along with the empire's ideology?

The one that won't bend the knee to Jezebel?

It's not eating in Israel.

It's eating in the unlikeliest places—places the religious elite would never expect.

God has a habit of **sending His prophets where the hunger is real.**

And sometimes? That means **eating pancakes in enemy territory.**

Ravens, Rivers, and the Widow's Last Meal

After Elijah drops the hard word on Ahab, he pulls an immediate Houdini and retreats to the wilderness, to a river of God's choosing, where he enters what can only be described as the first recorded instance of divine Uber Eats. Ravens—unclean birds, mind you—become his personal catering service, dropping off bread and meat twice daily, like a celestial Doordash, except with talons. Elijah, the rugged prophet, is now essentially being served room service by scavenger birds, which is both humiliating and, honestly, kind of metal.

This is peak **God's economy**—entirely irrational, totally upside-down, defying every expectation of how divine provision *should* work. If we were in charge, we'd set Elijah up with a robust, sustainable meal plan—perhaps an underground bunker with a six-month supply of grain, maybe a slow-roasted lamb every Tuesday. Instead? **God picks the most inconvenient, implausible, humiliating delivery system imaginable: carrion birds.**

And then, just when Elijah has gotten used to his bizarre wilderness routine, the river dries up. Because, well—**famine.** The very judgment Elijah called down is now knocking on his door, forcing him to move. And this is what most people don't realize about prophets: **You don't just deliver the hard word. You live it.**

From Ravens to a Starving Widow

God then gives Elijah a new plan—this time, a human will provide for him. A *widow* no less. Not a wealthy landowner, not an influential statesman—no, a woman scraping the bottom of survival, in a foreign land that *literally* worships the god Elijah has just publicly humiliated.

God tells Elijah:

"I have commanded a widow there to feed you."

Only one small problem: **God forgot to tell the widow.**

Elijah rolls into town expecting a warm meal, maybe a little hospitality. Instead, he's greeted by a woman gathering sticks—**the ancient Near Eastern equivalent of trying to find loose change in the couch cushions.** She's at the end of her rope, and when Elijah, bold as ever, asks for food, she hits him with what is arguably the *saddest* line in the Bible:

"I have only a handful of flour and a little oil. I was just gathering sticks to make a last meal for my son and me. Then we will eat it, and we will die."

Elijah's response?
"Go ahead and do that. But first, make me some pancakes."

You cannot make this up. The audacity. The complete and utter disregard for *optics*. If Twitter had existed in 850 BC, this would have been trending as #ElijahIsOverParty. The think pieces would write themselves:

- **"Elijah, the Religious Charlatan: How Men of God Exploit the Poor."**
- **"Why the Patriarchy Wants Your Last Meal: A Widow's Tale of Theocratic Oppression."**

The Invitation to the Miracle

On the surface, Elijah looks like the *worst* dinner guest of all time. The optics? Abysmal. But what he says next reframes the moment:

> **"For thus says the Lord, the God of Israel: The jar of flour shall not be spent, and the jug of oil shall not be empty, until the day the Lord sends rain on the land."**

This is the invitation to the miracle.

But notice—it's an *invitation,* not a handout.

Elijah does *not* say: *"Oh no, sweet widow! Keep your last meal— I'll find another way."* He also doesn't whip out a loaf of pre-miracled manna. Instead, **he asks her to risk everything—to bet her last meal on God's provision.**

And this is *exactly* why modern Evangelicalism is so *toothless.* Pastors want to give people comfort without the cost. They want to hand out grace like it's participation trophies at a Franklin soccer game—**no risk, no sacrifice, just good vibes and a "God loves you" sticker.**

But the **economy of God runs on faith.** The miracle is not *automatic.* It requires the *risk of faith.*

The Risk of Faith

The widow doesn't know Elijah. She doesn't know YHWH. She swears on *his* God, not hers. She is, by all accounts, a **total outsider.**
And yet, she bets her very *existence* on Elijah's word.

- She places her absolute last meal in God's hands.
- She brings **first** to God's prophet, trusting there will be something left for her and her son.
- And because of that?
  - **Her flour never runs out.**
  - **Her oil never dries up.**
  - **She and her son survive the famine.**

The **miracle follows the obedience.**
And this is the great, unspoken scandal of Western Christianity. We want **miracles without obedience.** We want **revival without repentance.** We want **God's supernatural provision without having to risk anything.** But faith is **not** a spiritual vending machine. **It is a radical bet on God's word,** even when every logical fiber of your being is screaming *Nope. Impossible. There's no way.*

God's Economy Runs on the Hard Word

This is what Jesus was hammering home in Luke 4.
When He preached in Nazareth, He reminded them:

> **"There were many widows in Israel in Elijah's time... yet Elijah was sent to none of them—only to a widow in Zarephath."**

Translation:

God is not obligated to provide for the entitled.

God is not obligated to work miracles for those who demand signs without faith.

God isn't handing out free lunch—He's *inviting people into a faith that costs something.*

The Three Sides of the Elijah Church

The Elijah Church exists in three realities in this story:

1. **Elijah at the Brook** – The Elijah Church is *supernaturally* provided for, even when the world is in famine. God feeds His own.
2. **Elijah at the Widow's House** – The Elijah Church delivers the **hard word** first, offering the invitation to miraculous provision *through faith.*
3. **The Widow** – The Elijah Church *bets everything* on the Word of the Lord.

This is **the paradox of divine provision.**

God will take care of His own—but not without demanding faith in return.

The question is: **Will we take the risk?**

Or will we clutch our last meal, hold onto our last drop of oil, convinced that God's economy is just as fragile and uncertain as the world's?

The Elijah Church takes the bet.

And **that's** where the miracle happens.

The Hard Word: The Prophetic Calling of the Church

For so many reasons—some valid, some eye-rollingly overblown—pastors have developed a debilitating phobia of giving people the *hard word* about their lives, their faith, and (most of all) their **finances**.

And I get it.

Nobody *wants* to be that guy. Nobody wants to be lumped in with the sweaty, gold-chain-wearing televangelists promising "a financial breakthrough" if you just sow a $777 seed offering **RIGHT NOW, DON'T DELAY, CALL THIS NUMBER, OH LOOK A PRAYER CLOTH!**

So, in our righteous desperation **not** to look like those guys, we overcorrected.

We became allergic to asking people to give. We started speaking in *apologetic tones* whenever we preached on finances. We overemphasized the abuses of prosperity preachers until we created an entirely *new* distortion: the **poverty gospel**—the unspoken assumption that money is inherently bad, and that giving generously is somehow *less spiritual* than just "being faithful with what you have."

And in doing so, we didn't just rob the Church of resources—we robbed **God's people** of an opportunity to activate their faith.

We closed a **point of access** to God that He actually wants **open.**

The Church as the Intersection of Heaven and Earth

One of the primary tasks of a pastor (or a prophet, or any true spiritual leader) is to function as a **pontifex**—literally, a "bridge-builder" between God and His people.

That's what Church is supposed to be:

- A **meeting place** between heaven and earth.
- A **sacred intersection** where the supernatural crashes into the natural.
- A **point of access** where God's presence becomes tangible, real, undeniable.

This is **Genesis 28**—Jacob's ladder.

Jacob falls asleep in the wilderness, dreams of a **stairway to heaven** (not the Led Zeppelin kind), wakes up completely freaked out, and declares:

> *"Surely this is the house of God! This is the gate of heaven!"*

That is what every church gathering should feel like.

It doesn't have to have TED Talk vibes with some Hillsong-esque music tearing your face off. Rather, **a gateway to heaven.**

And what **activates** that sacred intersection?

True worship.

Not just emotional sincerity.

Not just good vibes.

Not just closing your eyes and swaying like you're in a spiritual-themed Febreze commercial.

But **actual, tangible, physical sacrifice.**

Why God Asks for Something Physical

From **Genesis to Revelation**, God's pattern for worship is this:

1. **It must be what He asked for.**
2. **It must be the best of what He asked for.**

3. It must cost something.

Cain's offering was rejected because it wasn't **what God asked for.**

Israel's second-rate sacrifices were rejected because they weren't **the best.**

David refused to give anything to God that **didn't cost him something.**

Why is this such a big deal?

Because we are **physical** creatures, and our hearts are tied to **physical things.**

- Our money.
- Our possessions.
- Our resources.

These aren't just **stuff**—they represent survival. They represent security. They represent our ability to control our own futures.

And **that's** why giving is so powerful.

Because when we offer God what could sustain us, we are declaring:

"This thing does not keep me alive—YOU do."

That is **faith** in its rawest form.

Sacrifices Don't Save You—They Prove You're Saved

One of the biggest misunderstandings about **New Testament giving** is this idea that it somehow **earns** favor with God.

It doesn't.

In the Old Testament, sacrifices were required for **atonement.**

In the New Testament, sacrifices are the **evidence** of faith.

Big difference.

The widow of **Zarephath** wasn't saved **because** she gave Elijah food.

The widow in **Mark 12** wasn't saved **because** she put in two small coins.

These acts weren't **transactions**—they were **proof**.

Proof that these women believed the **Word of God** enough to bet everything on it.

Proof that **faith wasn't just intellectual assent, but embodied trust.**

The problem with modern Christianity?

We want **intellectual** faith with **zero risk.**

We want **assurance** without **obedience.**

We want **all the benefits of faith** without ever being asked to put something *on the altar.*

But that's not how the economy of God works.

- Faith is **tested.**
- Faith is **revealed through action.**
- Faith is **not faith until it costs you something.**

And when you step out in obedience—when you take the **risk of faith**—that's when you see God move.

That's when you realize **the flour will not run out.**

That's when you discover **the oil will not dry up.**

That's when you watch **God take care of you in ways you never imagined.**

The Pancake Church is faced with a choice.

Will it cling to what little it has left, hedging its bets, hoping to stretch its resources just a *little* longer—until it withers and dies?

Or will it **bet everything** on the hard word?

Will it have the audacity to say, **"God comes first, no matter what."**

The Elijah Church already knows the answer.

Pastors Who Rob Their People

Let me be blunt: **many pastors today are robbing their people.**
Not of money.
Not of tithe checks, building fund donations, or ATM withdrawals "for the kingdom."
But of **the invitation into God's supernatural supply.**
And why? Because they're scared.
Scared of being lumped in with the televangelist sociopaths, the seed-money hustlers, the prosperity snake-oil peddlers who talk more about private jets than personal holiness. They're terrified that **if they talk about giving, they'll sound like 90's Creflo Dollar after an espresso binge.**
So instead of teaching **the full counsel of God,** they just... don't. They backpedal, stay vague, and leave their congregations with half-truths and watered-down theology. They let fear set the agenda.

Elijah's "Really Bad Timing"

Let's be real: **Elijah had the absolute worst timing in the history of prophetic ministry.**
Imagine this scenario:
A single mom, starving. Her kid, wasting away. They're down to their final meal. And out of nowhere, **some bearded, wild-eyed prophet shows up at her door and says,**
"Hey, before you die... make me pancakes first."
That is a PR nightmare.
If Elijah were alive today, social media would have **a field day with this.**

"🔔 BREAKING: Religious Leader Demands Widow's Last Meal—Says 'God Told Him To' 🔔"

"#CancelElijah: Prophet Exploits Starving Woman"

"Televangelist Prophet Elijah Accused of Pancake Ponzi Scheme"

On the surface, **it looks like a scam.** It looks like the kind of abuse that people like Richard Dawkins drool over as proof that religion is a confidence trick played on the desperate.

Except, here's the twist: Elijah wasn't after her food.

He was after her faith.

Because the miracle was **on the other side of the hard word.**

Why Jesus Didn't Stop the Widow's Offering

Fast-forward to the New Testament.

Jesus is sitting in the temple, watching people drop money into the offering. Rich guys are making it rain. But then, **a poor widow walks up and puts in two pennies—everything she has.**

And what does Jesus do?

Nothing.

He doesn't stop her.

He doesn't say, "No, no, keep your money, you need it more than the temple does."

He doesn't pat her on the back and tell her, "God knows your heart—you don't need to give."

Instead, **He praises her.**

"She has given more than all of them."

Why? Because **she wasn't giving to an institution.** She wasn't "funding a ministry." She wasn't buying **God Points™** for future blessings.

She was entering into God's supernatural economy.

And Jesus, knowing exactly how this works, lets her step into it.

Because **the invitation into supernatural provision is never a robbery.**

Pastors, Stop Letting Hophni and Phinehas Set the Tone

Every generation has its religious scammers.

In the Old Testament, it was **Hophni and Phinehas**—two corrupt priests who stole from the people and turned worship into a racket.

In the New Testament, it was **the Pharisees**—self-righteous frauds who "devoured widows' houses" while praying long, sanctimonious prayers.

And today? **Yeah, we still have them.**

We have false teachers who turn tithing into extortion.

We have celebrity preachers who run the Church like a Wall Street hedge fund.

We have grifters who promise financial miracles while filling their **fifth** Swiss bank account.

But here's the thing:

Just because some people have abused the offering doesn't mean the offering itself is abusive.

Just because some men are **wicked in ministry** doesn't mean **the ministry itself is wicked.**

Imagine refusing to preach about prayer because some people use prayer manipulatively.

Imagine refusing to talk about marriage because some people abuse marriage.

Imagine refusing to teach about grace because some people use grace as a license to sin.

You **wouldn't.** Because **that's stupid.**

So why do so many pastors refuse to teach about giving **just because some heretics misused it?**

Be a Faithful Messenger—Not the Holy Spirit

Let me **free some pastors from their self-imposed anxiety:**
   You are not the Holy Spirit.
   You cannot **force conviction.**
   You cannot **manipulate obedience.**
   You cannot **manufacture faith.**
   You are **only responsible for delivering the Word.**
   If you give the hard word, and people reject it? **That's on them.**
   If you shrink back from giving the hard word, and your people **miss the invitation into God's provision? That's on you.**
   And God will hold you accountable for it.

The Elijah Church: Where Do We Stand?

At the end of the day, the Elijah Church is defined by **one thing: Faithfulness.**
   Faithful to deliver the hard word—even when the optics are bad.
   Faithful to trust God's provision—even when it seems impossible.
   Faithful to invite others into the miracle—even when they don't fully understand it yet.
   This **isn't** about money.
   This **isn't** about fundraising.
   This **is about trusting God's economy over man's economy.**
   And those who **bet their lives** on His Word—those who give Him **the first, the best, the everything—** will never lack what they need.

The **flour will not run out.**
The **oil will not dry up.**
And in every famine, in every crisis, in every impossible situation, **the faithful will see the miraculous hand of God.**

Chapter Eight

The Naaman Church

Naaman wanted healing, but he wanted it with **dignity**—the ceremonial, high-profile, red-carpet version of divine intervention. He had imagined something far grander, something befitting a man of his stature. Maybe a dramatic prayer session, an extravagant offering, a priestly parade where he could be *seen* receiving his miracle. At the very least, he expected Elisha to **show up in person**—maybe wave his hands, invoke the name of Yahweh in some elaborate ritual, and make a scene.

Instead, he got a *message* from a *servant* telling him to go dunk himself in **enemy water**. No spectacle. No grand spiritual performance. Just a prescription as undignified as the disease itself.

And that? That was the real insult.

Because Naaman, for all his desperation, still wanted to be *treated like a general*. He still wanted to receive healing in a way that preserved his **power, status, and personal pride**. He wanted the benefits of God, but on his **own cultural terms**—the same way we, today, want grace without repentance, forgiveness without transformation, **faith without surrender**.

And that's why the Naaman Church—the modern church that mirrors this entitled posture—so often fails to experience the miraculous.

It *wants* God, but it wants Him **conveniently**.

It *wants* healing, but it wants it **without obedience**.

It *wants* faith, but it wants it **without humility**.

Miracle Without a Show? Hard Pass.

The Naaman Church wants miracles, but not if they require humility. Not if they require trust. Not if they involve **Jordan River-level obedience**.

Instead, it wants spiritual **pageantry**—a faith that's **marketable, shareable, emotionally moving, and Instagrammable**. Something polished. Something cinematic. Something that doesn't feel embarrassing. Something that lets us maintain our *reputation* while still participating in *spirituality*.

But what if the healing is in something humiliating?

What if the miracle is in the mundane?

What if faithfulness means embracing **small obedience instead of grand experiences**?

Because here's the irony of Naaman's story:

He almost **missed his miracle** over the dumbest reason imaginable.

Not because the cure was impossible.

Not because the task was too difficult.

Not because the prophet refused to help.

He almost **chose leprosy** over **dipping himself in the wrong river**.

Pride Will Kill You First

Naaman didn't have an Assyrian problem.

He had a **pride problem**.

He could accept that he needed help. He could admit that he was dying. But he *could not* stomach the solution being **beneath him**.

This is where so many churches are today.

They recognize they are **spiritually sick**.

They see that the culture is **corrupt**.

They know the Western Church is **on life support**.

But when they are given **the remedy**?

When they are told to return to *biblical faithfulness*, to *historic Christianity*, to *obedience over innovation*?

They scoff.

"The Jordan? That dirty trickle?"

"Repentance? That outdated doctrine?"

"Holiness? That rigid legalism?"

"Biblical sexuality? That's oppressive!"

Like Naaman, they want **a better river**.

Something progressive. Something new. Something with **a TED Talk and a latte bar**.

They want an **Elisha with a PhD**.

They want **Christianity, but with cool branding and inclusive language**.

What they **don't** want?

The real thing.

Because the real thing looks like **dying to self**.

The real thing looks like **submission**.

The real thing looks like **humility**—even when it's *undignified*.

The Church That Finally Dipped

Naaman's servants, realizing that their master was about to let his *skin literally rot off* over wounded pride, **step in**.

They say, **"My father, if the prophet had told you to do some great thing, wouldn't you have done it? How much more when he tells you, 'Wash and be cleansed'?"** *(2 Kings 5:13)*

Translation:

"If Elisha had asked you to fight a war, you'd have done it. If he had told you to donate a palace, you'd have done it. If he had sent you on an impossible quest, you would have jumped at the chance to prove yourself."

"But because the only thing required of you is humility, you're walking away?"

That was the gut punch Naaman needed.

So, finally—probably grumbling, probably rolling his eyes, probably feeling **absolutely ridiculous**—he **dips himself** in the Jordan.

Once.

Twice.

Three times.

Still nothing.

Four times.

Five.

Still nothing.

Six.

Still nothing.

And then—on the seventh?

His skin is **restored like that of a young boy**.

He emerges, **healed**.

Because God doesn't owe you anything on the **first try**.

God doesn't owe you **immediate proof** that obedience is working.

God isn't a vending machine that dispenses **instant gratification**.

God honors faith. And faith is obedience **before you see the results**.

The Naaman Church Has a Choice

Right now, the Western Church is standing at the **edge of the Jordan**.

It has a choice:

1. Dip seven times, even when it looks pointless.

Or

2. Walk away and let the rot continue.

If we humble ourselves, **return to biblical faithfulness**, **stop craving popularity**, and **submit to God's ways instead of our own**, we will be healed.

If we **refuse**—if we hold onto our pride, if we keep chasing "better rivers," if we insist on keeping our *dignity intact*—we will **die in the disease**.

Because in the end, there are no "better rivers."

There is only **obedience or decay**.

And the Naaman Church must choose.

The Humility Factor: When a Warlord Takes Advice From His Interns

Naaman, the Assyrian warlord—battle-hardened, blood-soaked, and used to having men bow before him—is about to throw away his only shot at healing because of what can only be described as a *mild inconvenience*. His issue isn't that the cure is impossible; it's that it's *beneath him*. This isn't a battlefield conquest. This isn't a Herculean challenge. This isn't the kind of feat that makes bards write songs about you. It's a bath. Seven dips in a glorified puddle.

And that? That's the real insult.

But here's where the story takes a turn. His servants—the guys who polish his armor, feed his horses, and are quite literally paid to *shut up and follow orders*—step in.

They challenge him.

"My lord, if the prophet had told you to do something *difficult*, wouldn't you have done it? So why not do this *simple* thing?"

And Naaman? He listens.

That's what makes him different.

Not his military prowess.

Not his brute force.

Not even his desperation.

But his ability to hear correction *from those beneath him.*

Faith Without Humility Is Just a Religious Ego Trip

There's a lot of talk about faith these days. But faith without humility? That's just religious arrogance with a fresh coat of churchy paint.

Real faith says, *"I believe God."*

Real humility says, *"I believe God, even when it's inconvenient."*

Naaman *wanted* the miracle. He *believed* in the possibility of being healed. But the sticking point wasn't faith—it was humility. Could he submit to a process that felt stupid? Could he obey instructions that made *no sense*?

This is where modern people—especially modern church people—get tripped up.

They say they want *God's power* but don't want *His ways.*

They want the supernatural without submission.

They want divine wisdom without divine obedience.

They want miracles without method.

They want *God to speak*, but only through a medium they approve of—something TED Talk-y, podcast-friendly, aesthetically pleasing, and easy to digest.

They want spirituality, but not Scripture.

Essentially, they want to be their own prophet, priest, and king. They want a faith that never inconveniences them, never asks them to change, never demands that they wash in a muddy river when they know of *better rivers back home.*

And that's why so many never receive the miracle.

God Speaks Through the People We'd Rather Ignore

Naaman expected *the Prophet* to come out in a grand display—to wave his hands, call upon the heavens, and make it an *event.* Instead, he gets:

- A **slave girl**—a nobody in his house, a prisoner of war, who *should have hated him* but instead points him toward healing.
- A **foreign prophet**—who refuses to even come outside, doesn't flatter him, doesn't give him special VIP treatment.
- A **group of servants**—who confront his pride and, against all odds, save him from himself.

God doesn't show up in the form we prefer. He shows up in the form that demands *humility.*

Because, as the old saying goes: *There is no spiritual disease that humility cannot cure.*

Are We Willing to Listen?

I cannot count the number of times I've watched some social media pastor spiral into total self-parody. You know the ones—their YouTube thumbnails are just them screaming into a microphone, they've abandoned the Gospel in favor of algorithm-pleasing rage-bait, and every sermon sounds like an infomercial for their latest political vendetta.

And every time, I think the same thing:

This guy has no friends. No one in his life can tell him he's acting like a jackass. And that's because he's not humble.

That's the real test. Not your theology. Not your following. Not your "anointing."

Are there people in your life who can tell you when you're wrong?

Naaman—a *literal warlord*—listened to his servants. And because of that, he was healed.

The Naaman Church: A New Kind of Faith

The Naaman Church isn't defined by signs and wonders, prosperity, or even great acts of faith. It is a *church of humility*.

A church that:

- **Doesn't demand miracles on its own terms**—it follows God's process, even when it doesn't make sense.
- **Listens to correction from unexpected voices**—even when those voices are inconvenient, uncomfortable, or come from people we think are beneath us.
- **Refuses to be its own prophet, priest, and king**—submitting instead to God's actual Word, not just a curated version of it.

Because faith without humility? That's just self-delusion.
And God *resists* the proud.
But He *gives grace* to the humble.

The Naaman Church: Faith Inside the Empire

Now, here's where things get really interesting.

After Naaman is healed, he does something bizarre. He loads up his donkey with *dirt*—Israel's soil—to take back with him to Assyria.

At first glance, this seems like an odd, almost superstitious move. But this is an act of defiance.

Naaman is making a statement of faith.

He now belongs to YHWH, the God of Israel. And if *YHWH is God*, then Assyria's soil isn't really his *home* anymore.

This is the equivalent of a Roman centurion building a makeshift altar to Jesus inside a shrine to Mars. Or a high-ranking Soviet officer kneeling in prayer behind the Iron Curtain.

Naaman is *still inside the empire*—but he has *changed allegiances*.

And that's the problem. Because you can't serve two masters.

Faith in the empire is easy *until it clashes with the empire*.

The moment Naaman takes Israel's dirt home, he's broadcasting a theological bombshell: *YHWH reigns in Assyria, too.*

And if that's true, his entire world is about to get a lot more complicated.

But that's the nature of true conversion.

When you bow to the real God, you stop bowing to all the false ones.

And the empire *never* likes that.

Faith in the Midst of Compromise: The Naaman Dilemma

Naaman understands something that modern Christians often forget: faith rarely arrives in a vacuum. It does not land in a pristine, untangled, ideologically-pure life. No, faith crashes headlong into preexisting allegiances, prior commitments, and tangled moral complications. It disrupts, but it does not always immediately dismantle.

Naaman is still an Assyrian general.

He is still tethered to a brutal empire.

He still serves a pagan king who regularly bows before a statue of Ishtar.

And so, in an act of stunning theological honesty, Naaman lays his problem before Elisha:

> *"Look, I worship YHWH now, but I still have to operate within my political and military role. When my king bows to Ishtar, I have to be there. I have to kneel. I don't believe in it anymore, but I have to play the part. Is that okay?"*

And here comes the part that fries every rigid, legalistic, rule-bound theological circuit in the modern mind:

Elisha blesses him.

"Go in peace."

That's it.

No dramatic altar call.

No demand that Naaman quit his position.

No insistence that he dismantle systemic Assyrian oppression before his faith is considered legitimate.

Just *Go in peace.*

The Elisha Church: The Church That Gives the Hard Word

Elisha doesn't sugarcoat the message for Naaman. He doesn't round the edges. He doesn't package faith like a TED Talk, offering him a sleek, digestible, self-improvement plan. Naaman is given **one** requirement.

"Go wash in the Jordan seven times."

It's absurd. It's humiliating. And that's the whole point.

God isn't interested in our preferences. He does not workshop faith through a focus group. The demands of the Gospel are not up for revision every time a VIP walks in the door.

Naaman doesn't get a special exemption because of his rank. He doesn't get a different process because he's an elite general. He gets the same irrational, uncomfortable, deeply humbling command as any commoner.

Dip in the Jordan.

Not in Assyria's pristine rivers.

Not in a marble palace bath.

Not in a gilded ceremony with incense and chanting.

Just **dip in the Jordan**—the same river Israel's peasants used to water their livestock.

The Gospel is Not a Subscription Service

This is where the Elisha Church and the modern church part ways.

Because today's church? It's terrified of discomfort.

It will twist itself into a theological pretzel to make faith as accessible as possible. It will remove every ounce of tension, every requirement of obedience, every notion of submission. It will bend doctrine to make sure belief is easy, convenient, and free of any real cost.

And that's why modern Christianity has the spiritual tensile strength of wet cardboard.

Naaman doesn't get healed until he submits.

The widow doesn't get provision until she gives Elijah her last meal.

Peter doesn't walk on water until he steps out of the boat.

There is always a **faith act.**

There is always **a test of trust.**

And the Elisha Church refuses to rob people of that.

Faith Inside the Empire: A Crisis for Modern Christians

What do we do with Naaman?

Here we have a fully converted, YHWH-worshiping believer—who is still actively working for an empire that despises Israel.

He doesn't resign.

He doesn't become a political dissident.

He doesn't start a rebellion.

He doesn't withdraw into the hills, forming an Assyrian chapter of the Amish.

He simply believes.

And this, more than anything, is where modern Western Christians struggle. Because we love clean **binaries.**

We want clean-cut lines between the righteous and the wicked.

We want clear categories—oppressor vs. oppressed, good vs. evil, saint vs. sinner.

We want villains to publicly renounce their past, issue long-winded apologies, and step down from power before we'll accept their faith as real.

But **God doesn't play by those rules.**

He welcomes the Centurion without requiring him to defect from Rome.

He welcomes the tax collector without making him pay reparations first.

He welcomes Naaman, the Assyrian warlord, without demanding he dismantle Assyrian supremacy.

And that makes a lot of people very, very uncomfortable.

Jesus Doesn't Care About Your Marxist Narrative, Sweet Pea

Maybe—just maybe—God doesn't fit neatly into our Oppressor/Oppressed paradigm.

Maybe He doesn't share your Twitter feed's righteous indignation.

Maybe He's not interested in forcing every believer to issue a political repentance statement before their salvation can be considered legitimate.

Maybe grace is more offensive than we ever imagined.

Naaman remains a general.

The Centurion remains in the Roman army.

Neither is asked to step down, dismantle, or "deconstruct" their empire's hierarchy.

And yet?

Their faith is celebrated.

This is what the **Elisha Church** understands. It refuses to make faith easier than it should be, but it also refuses to make it harder than it needs to be. It gives the hard word—but **only the hard word that God actually gives.**

It does not require people to perform guilt theater.

It does not demand virtue-signaling apologies.

It does not impose ideological purity tests.

It simply declares:

"Believe. Obey. Dip in the Jordan."

And then?

"Go in peace."

The Naaman Church: Faith That Eats Empires

So what do we do with the **Naaman Church**?

Do we demand a more radical break from the systems of power?

Do we expect a total renunciation of their former ways?

Do we insist they publicly confess their participation in systemic injustice before we count them as *real* believers?

No.

We **thank God** for them.

Because God isn't in the business of **tearing down empires**.

He's in the business of **eating them from the inside out**—like divine termites gnawing at the foundations of human arrogance until the whole thing collapses under its own weight.

We forget this.

We assume Christianity must always be **oppositional**, always marching with protest signs, always trying to storm the gates of cultural strongholds with a battering ram. But historically? Christianity doesn't win **by revolution**. It wins **by infiltration**.

Rome didn't fall because Christians **overthrew** it.

Rome fell because Christians **infested** it.

They got into the government.

They got into the military.

They got into the economy, the arts, the philosophy, the **culture**—until the entire empire, once bent on **eradicating Christianity**, suddenly found itself **spreading Christianity** to the ends of the earth.

That's the playbook.

Not riots.

Not coups.

Not revolutions.

Just **faithful men and women living in the system, transforming it from the inside**.

→ **Naaman inside Assyria.**
→ **Centurions inside Rome.**
→ **Daniel inside Babylon.**

And suddenly? The Empire is working for the Gospel **without even realizing it**.

The Liturgies of Elisha

We **like to think** that encounters with Jesus automatically change people.

That someone hears the Gospel, has a nice spiritual epiphany, and—boom—instant transformation.

But what we actually see in Scripture?

People don't just have **love encounters** with God.

They have **truth encounters** and **power encounters**—and **without all three, faith is just sentimentality.**

→ Naaman had a **love encounter**—he was **welcomed**, despite being a brutal enemy.

→ Naaman had a **truth encounter**—God's ways were **not negotiable**; he had to **dip in the Jordan**, not Assyria's rivers.
→ Naaman had a **power encounter**—his body was **physically healed**; his faith was backed by **supernatural reality**.

The **modern church** loves the love encounter.
But we downplay the truth and power encounters.
We whisper about **truth**, hoping nobody notices.
We downplay **power**, because we're afraid of looking weird.
We offer **Christianity without cost, without confrontation, without conviction**—a vague *spirituality* where God loves you but demands nothing, where Jesus is your homeboy but not your King.
But **faith** isn't just a **warm feeling**.
It's an **action**.

→ It's **washing in the Jordan seven times** when it doesn't make sense.
→ It's **bringing your last meal to Elijah before you eat it yourself**.
→ It's **stepping out of the boat when Jesus calls**.

If there's **no power encounter**, there's no real transformation.
If there's **no truth encounter**, there's no real conversion.
And if we don't **preach the full Gospel**, we aren't actually preaching **anything** at all.

The Church the World Needs

The world is too broken for safe churches.
People are walking in with **sexual confusion, deep trauma, broken identities, and shattered worldviews**.
They don't need **a TED Talk church**.

They don't need **a sanitized, non-offensive, 20-minute sermon** with a cool title slide.

They don't need **three points and a poem**.

They need **the power of God**.

They need **a church that doesn't flinch**.

They need **a church that doesn't apologize for Scripture**.

They need **a church that doesn't bow to the empire but infiltrates it**.

The Naaman Church Eats Culture Alive

You know what *actually* changes the world?

It's not culture war outrage.

It's not fighting about boycotts on Twitter.

It's not memes dunking on progressives or conservatives or whatever tribe you think is ruining everything.

It's **a man like Naaman**, who goes home to his pagan city, with his pagan job, and quietly starts **serving YHWH anyway**.

It's **a Roman Centurion**, who never leaves the army, but starts serving **Jesus as Lord instead of Caesar**.

It's **Esther**, who doesn't quit the palace, but **uses her position to save her people**.

It's **Joseph**, who doesn't tear down Pharaoh's system but **manages it better than Pharaoh ever could**.

That's how the **Kingdom of God wins**.

It eats empires alive.

It gets into the bloodstream of the culture, hijacks the **very thing meant to destroy it**, and turns it into the instrument of its own destruction.

Jesus doesn't need to burn down your empire.

He just needs **a few believers inside it**.

And the Naaman Church **is ready**.

Chapter Nine
Sticky Tucky Pointy

The Great Canadian Draft System

Growing up in Canada, we played street hockey year-round—rain or shine, snow or slush, mild frostbite be damned. If your fingers still functioned enough to hold a stick, the game went on. If they didn't, well, that's what yelling was for.

But assembling teams was an art. And, like everything in Canada, we tried to be fair about it. We mythologized fairness. We institutionalized fairness. We prayed to fairness like it was some sacred, benevolent deity.

Enter the Hockey Stick Draft System™.

Here's how it worked: Every player threw their hockey stick into a pile, a ceremonial offering to the gods of street justice. One lucky kid—a post-pubescent oracle—was chosen to kneel, blindfolded by another kid standing behind him, while a neutral party randomly chucked sticks left and right to form two teams.

A beautiful, democratic, fair system.

That was completely rigged.

Because, inevitably, the teams were stacked, and some unlucky soul got shuffled to the other side so things were "competitive." That's how fairness really works—it's not about ensuring balance; it's about making sure the weak aren't *too* miserable. It's the illusion of parity, a consolation prize for the athletically hopeless.

The Ruthless Efficiency of the Baseball Method

Compare that to America's Baseball Selection Method, which is brutally honest and soul-crushingly efficient.

Two team captains.

A public lineup of raw human worth.

The slow, methodical choosing of the strongest, the fastest, the biggest winners.

And—on the other end—the gut-wrenching death march of rejection.

For me? It was a familiar experience. I was small, slow, and strategically avoided until the very end, standing there like a human liability in sneakers, hoping against hope that today, miraculously, I had somehow gained superpowers.

Which means that I got tough fast.

By the time I was old enough to understand the real world, I had already learned the most crucial life lesson:

Some people are just better than you.

Some people are faster, taller, stronger, smarter.

Some people are chosen first.

And some people—like me—barely make the cut.

And I accepted that. I had to. That was the game. That was the deal.

Which is why when God started picking teams, I was floored.

Because God does not pick teams like I pick teams.

God's Upside-Down Draft Picks

If I were God, I wouldn't have picked me.

I wouldn't have picked any of the people He picks.

But Paul, in a letter to the Corinthians, reminds them:

"Not many of you were wise according to worldly standards. Not many were powerful. Not many were of noble birth. But God chose what is foolish in the world to shame the wise." (1 Cor. 1:26-27)

Translation:

"Hey guys—just so we're clear—most of you were total nobodies. Absolute morons. No offense."

Imagine reading that letter in church:
"Hey, uh, thanks Paul? I think?"
But Paul is dead serious.
Because God picks the people no one else would pick.
The Corinthians? A ragtag band of ex-slaves, hustlers, and broke merchants who had stumbled into wealth after Corinth became an economic boomtown.
This was a riotous, debauched, Las Vegas-on-the-Mediterranean city.
And God chose them.
He took the lowest of the low, the most unqualified, the most disreputable, and built a church.
Because this is God's thing. This is His brand. He is not the deity of the first-round draft picks. He is the patron saint of the benchwarmers, the third-string nobodies, the ones nobody trades for in fantasy leagues.
And this hits home for me.

My Almost-Trailer-Trash Testimony

Because my family?
We were barely not trailer trash.

Like, if trailer trash had a junior varsity league, we were in it. We were **trailer-adjacent**.

My uncles? Criminal records.

My dad? A drugged-out hippie, fresh off a trial for dealing drugs.

My ancestors? A glorious cocktail of Irish, Italian, and English peasantry, all scraping by in a former penal colony (thanks, Canada).

By every conceivable metric, my family should be a historical footnote—a cautionary tale, not a testimony.

But God laughed and picked us anyway.

And that's the joke.

Not just that God chooses the foolish, but that He delights in it. He *leans* into it. It's almost like He enjoys messing with the system, like a cosmic trickster who gets a perverse thrill out of watching the captains of the world realize their first-round picks are useless, and their last-round throwaways are running the show.

It's the divine equivalent of watching a billionaire's trust-fund kid fail spectacularly while some nobody from a two-stoplight town ends up revolutionizing an industry.

It's the great reversal. The cosmic uno-reverse. The upside-down draft pick.

And that? That's grace.

Grace is not meritocracy. It is not fairness. It is not the Hockey Stick Draft System™ where the strong and the weak are gently rearranged to create a tolerable illusion of equality.

Grace is God looking at the last, the least, the forgotten—me, my family, the Corinthians—and saying:

"You? You're my first pick."

Sticky: Moses and His Best Friend, A Stick

Moses is the ultimate bad draft pick.

By the time God calls him, he's an old man, a fugitive, a failed prince, and a despised shepherd. That's already a tough résumé to sell, but let's pile on: He's been out of the game for decades, marinating in the crushing obscurity of the Midianite desert, herding sheep that aren't even his. He's not even an independent failure—he's a franchise failure, running a team he doesn't own.

And, like Tom Hanks talking to Wilson the volleyball in *Cast Away*, Moses has probably spent way too much time talking to his staff—let's call it Sticky.

Now, Sticky isn't just a stick.

Sticky is a relic of Moses's downward spiral, a sad, splintered emblem of his fall from power. Sticky represents the gap between his younger, self-important, palace-dwelling past and his current reality as a desert nobody. Sticky is the trophy you get when life hands you third place and tells you, *"Just be grateful you placed at all."*

So when God calls Moses to confront Pharaoh, Moses panics. His objections come fast and anxious, a rapid-fire list of why he is a terrible choice:

"I'm old. I can't talk. I have no credibility. My best friend is a stick. You picked the wrong guy."

And God—who, I assume, is holding back a grin—asks:

"What's in your hand?"

Moses looks down.

"Sticky."
"Throw Sticky on the ground."

Moses does.

Sticky becomes a snake.

And Moses runs for his life—because, of course, this guy is also terrified of snakes.

So let's review:

- ✔ Old as dirt
- ✔ Can't talk
- ✔ Lives in exile
- ✔ No leadership credentials
- ✔ Afraid of snakes
- ✔ Best friend is a stick

And this is the guy God picks to lead a revolution.

And Sticky—the symbol of Moses's failure—becomes the instrument of power.

Sticky will split the Red Sea.

Sticky will turn the Nile to blood.

Sticky will strike the rock for water.

Sticky will become a snake that eats other snakes.

God takes the most humiliating part of Moses's life and makes it His weapon.

And that's the redemptive pattern.

God's Draft Strategy: Losers First

When God builds His Church, He doesn't go for the Brad-Jamal-Todd power trio. He's not assembling the divine equivalent of a championship fantasy football team.

He picks the last kid on the fence.

He picks the runt, the outcast, the one everyone overlooked.

He picks a washed-up prince with a speech impediment and a stick.

And then—*this* is the crucial part—He doesn't fix them in the ways you'd expect. He doesn't turn Moses into a charismatic, silver-tongued leader. He doesn't set him up with a *TED Talk: How to Negotiate with Pharaoh Like a Boss*. He doesn't enroll him in a Toastmasters public speaking seminar.

He just gives him Sticky.

And that's the joke.

Because God doesn't need Moses to be strong. He needs him to be obedient.

Your Sticky, My Sticky, Everyone's Sticky

We all have a Sticky—some part of our life we consider an embarrassment, a failure, or a weakness. Something that reminds us of where we *aren't* and where we *never* wanted to be.

And God says, *"Perfect. I can use that."*

Because the foolish things shame the wise.

Because the weak things shame the strong.

Because the last will be first.

Because God builds His Kingdom on the backs of losers.

And that's good news.

Because it means even people like me have a shot.

Tucky: The Deadly Art of Blanket Hospitality

The story of Jael in *Judges* is one of the most underrated assassinations in history.

And that's saying something, because the Bible has **a lot** of assassinations. Stabbings, beheadings, people falling out of windows—*Game of Thrones* wishes it had this level of intrigue. But Jael? She goes about it with the quiet, slow-burn patience of a woman who's been waiting for *years* to do something like this.

Let's set the scene:

She is a total nobody. No backstory. No qualifications. Just a regular Israelite woman living in a tent during a time of war.

The bad guy? Sisera—the enemy general—who's on the run after the Lord flips the battle against him. He's scrambling, desperate, looking for a place to hide.

Jael spots him.

And she plays it cool.

Like a gracious and hospitable hostess, she greets him warmly and invites him into her tent.

"Come in, my lord, relax, put your feet up—would you like a snack?"

She tucks him in.

Blankets? Check.

Warm milk? Check.

Comfort and security? Check.

Sisera, exhausted, lets his guard down. The warm milk works its sleepy magic, the blankets cradle him in coziness, and he drifts off into dreamland.

And then?

Jael finds a **tent peg** and a **hammer**.

Moves softly to where Sisera is snoring.

Places the **tent peg** at his temple.

Swings the hammer.

Drives the peg **straight through his skull**.

Into the ground.

And then the narrator—bless him—adds:

"…So he died."

(Thanks for the **clarification**, Bible. Wasn't sure if the guy with a railroad spike through his head might pull through.)

Now, let's analyze the logistics of this.

Jael didn't have a sword.

Jael didn't have military training.

Jael wasn't a warrior.

She just had **Tucky Tucky skills**—and a tent peg.

And with Tucky and Pointy, God delivered Israel.

This should tell you something about how God works.

Because while we tend to picture divine power as thunderbolts and miracles, sometimes it's just a woman with a blanket, a steady hand, and the audacity to swing a hammer at the right moment.

Which means, if you feel like a nobody, if you feel like you've got nothing special to offer—no pedigree, no platform, no polished résumé—congratulations.

You might just be God's next first-round draft pick.

Pointy: Shamgar's Zero-Innovation Slaughterhouse

Even more obscure than Jael is Shamgar, an Israelite judge whose entire biblical résumé consists of exactly one verse:

> *"He killed 600 Philistines with an ox-goad."* (Judges 3:31)

That's it.

No context.

No backstory.

Just 600 dudes who got taken out with a *pointy stick*.

Now, an ox-goad is not a weapon. It is not a sword, a spear, or even a particularly menacing club. It's a glorified cattle prod—a long, wooden pole with a sharpened end, designed for poking large, stubborn livestock into compliance.

And yet, Shamgar—with nothing but this farm implement and, presumably, a really bad attitude—single-handedly slaughters *600* Philistines.

Let's pause and appreciate the absolute absurdity of this.

These Philistines? Armed to the teeth. Swords, shields, bronze weaponry, tactical formations.

Shamgar? Had a *stick*.

And he still won.

This is not just improbable—it's embarrassing. For the Philistines, I mean. Imagine being the 600th guy in line, watching 599 of your comrades go down, one after another, to some furious Israeli farmer wielding a *sharp stick*, and still thinking, *Yeah, I got this.*

You did not "got this."

And so Shamgar joins the ever-growing list of biblical nobodies who defy the odds using things that, by all reasonable metrics, should not be deadly.

Which leads us to the real mystery:

Why is God's recruitment process so *weird*?

God's Anti-Avengers Draft Strategy

If I were assembling the Bible X-Men, I would not be doing it this way.

I would recruit *heavy hitters*:

- **Clark Kent.** Can fly, super strength, bulletproof. You're in.
- **Peter Parker.** Radioactive spider powers, webs, agility. You're in.

- **Bruce Wayne.** Rich, father wound. Classic combo. You're in.

Then, some biblical tryouts:

- **Moses.**

"What's your skill?"
"I have a stick. His name is Sticky."
"...Yeah, pass."

- **Jael.**

"What's your deal?"
"Tucky."
"Hard no."

- **Shamgar.**

"And you?"
"Pointy stick."
"...Who invited these losers? This is hero tryouts, people!"
And yet?
God chooses them.

Not because they're the most skilled, the strongest, or the most intimidating—He picks them because they're the kind of people nobody else would pick.

Because when God wins using nobodies with everyday objects, it becomes abundantly clear that *He's* the one doing the winning.

The Unexpected Gifts God Uses

I grew up in rural Canada in the '90s.

And let me tell you, playing video games in the '90s was **not cool**.

In my high school, you had three social categories:

1. **The Hicks.** Drove trucks, listened to country music, wore camo unironically.
2. **The Jocks.** Played sports, had girlfriends, peaked early.
3. **The Druggies.** Skateboarded, listened to Metallica, failed algebra.

I hung out with the Jocks because I was funny. That was my currency.

But I could never, *never* tell them I was a gamer. That was social suicide. That was how you secured yourself a locker-stuffing.

So I kept my *GoldenEye 007* skills a secret.

But years later, when I moved back home to Canada and became a youth pastor, I was struggling to connect with the local kids. I tried everything—earnest conversations, cool events, pizza bribes.

Nothing worked.

Then one day, I overheard a group of 11-year-old goth weirdos talking about *Call of Duty*.

"You guys game?"

"Pchyeah."

"You play Call of Duty?"

"Pchyeah, man. Do you?"

"I dabble."

(I didn't *dabble*. I was a *monster*. A **digital executioner**. I struck fear into lobbies across the nation.)

So I invited them over for a gaming night.

And I *destroyed* them. No mercy. **Total annihilation**. I talked *so much* trash.

They *loved* it.

Then? They started coming to youth group.

Then? They brought their friends.

Then? **168 kids.**

Because of *video games*.

Something I was embarrassed about—something I had hidden because it didn't "fit" my idea of what God could use—became the very thing that connected me to the kids I was supposed to reach.

God Can Use Anything. Literally Anything.

We disqualify ourselves for the dumbest reasons.

"God can't use me—I'm not a TikTok influencer."

"I don't know how to make viral Christian content."

"I'm not funny, or cool, or social."

Lies.

God put you together **exactly** as you are.

He knows your quirks.

He knows your strengths and weaknesses.

He knows your weird, random talents.

And He will use them.

If He can use a *tent peg*, a *pointy stick*, and a *shepherd's staff*—if He can use *warm milk and a blanket* to defeat an army—then He can use you.

Because God doesn't need **better people**. He just needs **available people**.

And honestly? That's the best news ever.

Because it means you—yes, *you*, the one reading this right now—are already qualified.

The Secret of the Church: Surrendered Weakness

The **real power of the Church** isn't in **innovation** or **strategy**.
It's in **surrendered weakness**.
"Not by might, nor by power, but by My Spirit, says the Lord."
The **first-century church** was not **a group of elite theologians, influencers, and entrepreneurs**.
It was **fishermen, tax collectors, and ex-prostitutes**.
The **only thing they had in common**?
They **laid down their lives**.
They **trusted God to work through them**.
And that was **enough**.
Because **it's never been about us anyway**.
God **does not need influencers**.
God **does not need innovation**.
God **does not need talent**.
God just needs **Sticky, Tucky, and Pointy people**—people with **no confidence in themselves** and **every confidence in a miracle-working God**.

Final Thought: What's in Your Hand?

When Moses **panicked about his calling**, God didn't ask him for **a skillset or a strategy**.
He asked:
"What's in your hand?"
Moses looked down.
"...Sticky."
And that was enough.

Chapter Ten

The Future Church

The pastor of the church I grew up in was formerly Pentecostal but had left the Pentecostal Assemblies of Canada in the '60s over his father's embrace of Charismatic worship and expressions of the gifts of the Spirit in worship—namely, "the song of the Lord" and other prophetic manifestations that, to your average Canadian Protestant, sounded like a pack of wolves learning to harmonize.

We weren't dispensational at all—we believed that the Church was going to thrive in the Last Days, not limp into the eschaton like an injured deer looking for a place to die. We rejected the idea that God was a polygamist, maintaining two separate but unequal wives—Israel, the true love, His Rachel; and the Church, the spiritually obligated consolation prize, His Leah. We didn't buy into the secret rapture doctrine that insisted Jesus would beam up all the good boys and girls before things got a little dicey down here, leaving the poor, clueless world to fumble around trying to make sense of driverless cars and pilotless planes like an eschatological version of *The Purge*.

I remember going to Bethel Pentecostal Church in Hamilton, Ontario, as a kid one Sunday night with my family. I was around 11 or 12, and Bethel had decided to host a movie night in their parking lot—drive-in style. The film of choice? *Left Behind*. And let me tell you, seeing a lawnmower keep running after its owner had been sucked up into the great unknown was hilarious to my father. He cackled so loudly that I think we got a few side-eyes from the serious prophecy enthusiasts in attendance, the ones clutching their Scofield Reference Bibles like life vests.

Afterward, on the drive home, my dad started his usual post-service analysis, a little sermon of his own. *The problem,* he told me as I braced for one of his infamous diatribes, *with dispensationalism is that it's entirely pessimistic about the Church. It leads Christians to believe that they'll be white-knuckling their way to the finish line, just trying to survive until Jesus rescues them. But Jesus told us that it's the gates of hell that are white-knuckling, not the Church.*

My dad had a way of turning every theological discussion into a sports metaphor. *It's like we're supposed to be playing offense, but dispensationalists think we're running out the clock, playing not to lose.*

Years later, I'd sit in a chapel at Portland Bible College—up in the balcony, which was unofficially reserved for the late, the disillusioned, and the cool kids who could afford to be both—and I'd hear Kevin Conner articulate the same concept in a much more theologically dense manner:

"Your ecclesiology affects your eschatology, and your eschatology affects your ecclesiology."

Translation: What you believe about the End Times absolutely informs how you view the Church, and what you believe about the Church absolutely informs how you view the End Times. If you think the Church is doomed to fail, then you'll inevitably see the End Times as a divine cleanup job. If you believe the Church is a victorious, global movement, you'll see the return of Christ as the culmination of something glorious rather than a Hail Mary for a losing team.

The difference is everything.

One version of Christianity wakes up every morning expecting the world to get worse, gripping a tattered newspaper, frantically cross-referencing today's headlines with *Revelation,* and waiting for the Antichrist to start a TikTok account. The other version sees every moment as an opportunity for the Kingdom to break in, for renewal, for transformation, for the Church to expand into the very places that once seemed unredeemable.

So for clarity's sake, here's my stance:

I believe in a Church that is *raiding hell* until the loud, triumphant, and singular return of Christ.

I believe that there is *one* People of God now—Jews and Gentiles incorporated by faith into the Body of Christ—for whom Jesus is returning. When He comes back, He's not sneaking in like a divine cat burglar. He's arriving with fanfare, raising the dead, and recreating the world in a way that will make every CGI-heavy apocalyptic movie look like a preschool puppet show.

I believe Jesus is actively superintending the Church, His Bride, His Body, and this is His great work right now. And contrary to popular belief, I don't think Jesus sucks at His job.

And if Jesus is coming back for a *pure and spotless Bride*, then we have some theological reconfiguring to do. Because He's not coming back for some 700-pound loser that is overfed, under-exercised, spiritually comatose, and emotionally dependent on Hallmark movies and pudding cups. Neither is He returning for a weak, anemic, barely-breathing skeleton who looks like she just crawled out of a Victorian-era sanatorium.

No. The Church is alive. She is vibrant. She is growing. She is learning. She is making mistakes, yes, but she is also rising.

And if you still think the Church is on its last leg, just give it a minute. Because the same Spirit that raised Christ from the dead is still animating His people, still renewing the world, still kicking down the gates of hell.

And last I checked, *He doesn't lose.*

The Future Church: Five Pillars of an Unstoppable Movement

If the Church were a car, let's be real—it's been through some **things**. It's been a Ferrari, an old station wagon, a military tank, and, at times, a clown car with too many people honking the horn but no one driving. It's been an unstoppable force that shaped civilization and, in some eras, a bloated institution trying to figure out if it still had anything to say. But here's the thing: **Jesus is still in the driver's seat.** And He's not returning for some busted-up, barely-running jalopy held together by zip ties and theological duct tape. He's coming back for a **glorious** Bride. A thriving, beautiful, powerful Church that knows who she is and what she's about.

So what does this Future Church look like? **I believe it has five defining features.**

1. Presence Driven—We're Here for Jesus, Not Just Another Sunday™

I recently heard someone say, *"If all we're doing as a church is having another Sunday, it's pointless."* And I felt that. Deep in my bones. Because I don't know about you, but I **don't need another religious routine**. I don't need another three-song setlist followed by a sermon that sounds like it was written by ChatGPT and ends with some vague, existential encouragement about how I'm doing *great, sweetie*. I need **God**.

The **Future Church gathers for one reason: Jesus.** We're not gathering for hype, social networking, or to make sure Grandma doesn't call us on Sunday afternoon to passive-aggressively ask if we *skipped church again*. We are gathering **for Christ, through Christ, and because of Christ.**

This means that worship isn't performance-driven—it's *presence-driven*. It means that **prayer isn't a transition between worship and preaching—it's the main event.** It means that we aren't showing up to feel a vague sense of spirituality; we are showing up to **meet God in the room.**

We are **Mary first, Martha later.**

(And for the record, that doesn't mean we never do the work—it just means we sit at Jesus' feet before we start stress-cleaning the house like we're trying to impress God with our spiritual productivity.)

The Future Church is one where **Jesus is the point**, not just a talking point.

2. Kingdom Manifesting—We Expect the Real Thing, Not Just Churchy Vibes

Here's the problem with a lot of modern Christianity: **we are weirdly allergic to the supernatural.** And it makes **no** sense. If we actually believe that Jesus **died, was dead for three days, and then got up like it was nothing,** why do we struggle so hard to believe in miracles today?

The Future Church doesn't just believe in the Kingdom of God—it manifests it.

This means that where Jesus is, **the Kingdom breaks in.** When the King is present, His rule is evident. When Jesus showed up in Scripture, He didn't just give people a **pat on the back** and tell them to *do better*. He cast out demons. He healed the sick. He opened blind eyes and deaf ears. He raised dead people who had **already started smelling**. The Kingdom of God is not **metaphorical**. It is not **hypothetical**. It is **supernatural**.

We don't seek miracles for the sake of miracles. But we *do* seek the **King**—and the King **does** miracles. The Kingdom is not a

TED Talk. It is **power.** The Future Church is one that **actually expects God to do God-things**—not just for the sake of theatrics, but because when Jesus walks in the room, *stuff happens.*

3. Saint Equipping—No More Spiritual Infants at 40

Look, I love a good sermon. I love great teaching. But let's be honest—**some people have been in church for 20 years and still don't know how to feed themselves spiritually.**

The Future Church does **not** cater to perpetual spiritual toddlers.

It's a **Church of Disciples**, not **spiritual coasters** who show up, consume, and go home unchanged. The **mission of the Church is not just to make converts—it's to make disciples.** People who know **Scripture.** People who know **doctrine.**People who know **why they believe what they believe.**

We live in the **Age of Lawlessness**, where everyone has an opinion on what Christianity *should* be but **very few people actually read their Bibles.** (I mean, it's kind of a problem when people are basing their theology off TikTok influencers named @ PropheticBabe777.)

So, the **Future Church has to be serious about equipping people with the Word.**

It's not about **Bible nerds vs. "spirit people"**. It's **both.** We need Scripture and the Spirit. We need **people who love the Bible and know how to hear the voice of God.**

The days of **spiritual malnutrition are over.** The Future Church is a **training ground, not a daycare.**

4. World Reaching—No More Evangelical Witness Protection Program

At some point, we decided **evangelism was cringe.** Probably because we grew up watching those 90s "witnessing" methods where a youth pastor made us practice asking strangers, *"If you died tonight, do you know where you would go?"* (usually in a mall food court, where they were just trying to eat their Cinnabon in peace).

But **real** evangelism isn't a script. It's **real people bringing real Jesus to real life.**

The Future Church is **unashamed of the Gospel.** We don't need to trick people into salvation like we're selling timeshares in heaven. We just need to show them **the actual Jesus**—and that happens **through us.**

And guess what? **The Gospel is still good news.** It is still the **only** thing that saves, transforms, and redeems.

The Future Church doesn't **shy away from the truth** because of cultural discomfort. It **boldly holds up the moral mirror** and **offers a way of escape**—Christ Jesus.

We are done with **hiding.** The world needs hope, and we're done acting like we don't have it.

5. World Impacting—Enough With the Christian Irrelevance

There was a time when **the Church led the world in art, science, philosophy, and politics.** You know, **the Renaissance.** And yet today, we have settled for **irrelevance**, as if we are called to **retreat** instead of **lead.**

The Future Church is not **separate from culture**—it **shapes** culture.

We need **Christian leaders** in every sphere of influence. We need **filmmakers** who tell stories with excellence. We need **musicians** who make real art, not just Christian remixes of whatever the world did five years ago. We need **politicians** with conviction, **entrepreneurs** with Kingdom vision, and **thinkers** who aren't afraid of real intellectual engagement.

We need **another Constantine Moment**—a time when the Church rises up and **beautifies and preserves the world** instead of watching it burn.

The Future Church is **not a social club.** It's a **force.** It is **the answer the world doesn't know it's looking for.**

Epilogue
The Remnant and the Reckoning

The thing about history—real history, not the Twitter-thread version—is that it has a long memory. Civilizations rise, civilizations fall, and despite our collective amnesia, the pattern is never all that surprising. One empire gets too cocky, forgets the disciplines that made it great, and crumbles under the weight of its own hubris. Another emerges, eager, hungry, disciplined—until, of course, it isn't. The cycle repeats. The Greeks had their day. Rome had its run. The British took a lap around the globe. And now, here we are—living in the moment where the West, drunk on its own self-importance, has begun mistaking its decadence for progress.

But the real question—one far more relevant to the reader who has slogged through these pages—is this: Where does the Church fit into this cycle? Because the Church, unlike the civilizations it has outlived, is not an empire. It does not operate by brute force, nor does it collapse under the same weight of luxury and laziness that dooms every other human institution. The Church is different, or at least it's supposed to be. It's the thing that survives the wreckage. The thing that rises from the rubble. The thing that—if history is to be trusted—will remain long after today's self-proclaimed moral revolutionaries are reduced to an archaeological footnote.

And yet, let's be honest. If we were to judge the Church today solely by its Western expression—if we mistook the trendy, latte-drinking, TED Talk-giving, brand-conscious, algorithmically optimized version of Christianity as its totality—we might be tempted to say, "Well, maybe this time is different. Maybe this is the end." Maybe the Church has finally lost itself in the labyrinth of cultural compromise. Maybe, for the first time in history, the gates of hell have figured out how to prevail.

Except they haven't.

Because while much of the Church has gone soft—while entire denominations are in free fall, while Christian leaders are busy taking selfies with the spirit of the age—the real Church, the Joseph Church, is still here. It's still standing, still faithful, still quietly doing the thing it has always done. It is not the one making headlines. It is not the one getting invited to panels on "rethinking faith in a modern age." It is not the one trend-jacking social justice movements to get more engagement on Instagram. It is the one that is still singing when no one is watching. The one that is still preaching when the seats are empty. The one that is still opening the Word and declaring what God has actually said, not what a fickle culture wishes He had said.

This is what people forget. The collapse of one version of Christianity does not mean the collapse of the Church. Babel always falls. Joseph always rises. And while the modern, institutionalized, Western version of Christianity might be in a tailspin, the Church—the real one—is not worried.

If history has taught us anything, it is that God has no problem letting corrupted systems fall. He will not rescue a compromised Church from the consequences of its own cowardice. He will not prop up institutions that have become Babel 2.0, building towers in His name while using bricks borrowed from secularism. He will not bless that which is ashamed of Him.

But He will preserve a remnant.

He always does.

The remnant is not the loudest. It is not the wealthiest. It is not the best-marketed. It is not the one with publishing deals or CNN interviews or a seat at the table of cultural influence. But it is the one that survives. The one that thrives. The one that—when all of this nonsense comes crashing down—will still be standing.

Because God is not in the business of failure.

So yes—Western Christianity, as we know it, may very well collapse. But the Church? The real one? The one that fears God more than man? The one that sees through the lies and refuses to bow? The one that remembers where this all started and where it is all headed?

That Church is just getting started.

It's been here before.

It will be here long after we're gone.

And it will be here when the towers of this age come crashing down, when the ideological Babels of our time crumble into dust, when the fickle rulers of this world fade into irrelevance, when history—real history—has the final word.

The question is not whether the Church will endure.

The question is whether you will be part of the remnant that does.

BIBLIOGRAPHY

1. Chesterton, G.K. *Orthodoxy*. Ignatius Press, 1995, p. 200
2. Smith, James K.A. *You Are What You Love: The Spiritual Power of Habit*. Grand Rapids, MI: Brazos Press, 2016.
3. www.alastairadversaria.com/2018/01/19/jordan-peterson-and-powerful-men
4. Bruce, F.F. *The Early Church*. Grand Rapids, MI: Eerdmans, 1983.
5. Peretti, Frank E. Monster. Nashville, TN: Thomas Nelson, 2005